Y0-CBI-001

JUNG AND THE INTERPRETATION OF THE BIBLE

JUNG

AND THE INTERPRETATION OF

THE BIBLE

Edited by
✻ **David L. Miller** ✻

CONTINUUM • NEW YORK

1995
The Continuum Publishing Company
370 Lexington Avenue
New York, NY 10017

Copyright © 1995 by The Continuum Publishing Company

All rights reserved. No part of this book may be reproduced,
stored in a retrieval system, or transmitted, in any form or by
any means, electronic, mechanical, photocopying, recording, or
otherwise, without the written permission of The Continuum
Publishing Company.

Printed in the United States of America

Library of Congress Cataloging-in-Publication Data

Jung and the interpretation of the Bible / edited by David L. Miller.
     p. cm.
   Includes bibliographical references (p.).
   ISBN 0-8264-0809-5 (hbd)
   1. Bible—Criticism, interpretation, etc. 2. Bible—Psychology.
3. Jung, C. G. (Carl Gustav), 1875–1961. 4. Psychoanalysis and
religion. I. Miller, David LeRoy.

BS645.J86 1995   94-42560
220.6'01'9—dc20   CIP

CONTENTS

ACKNOWLEDGMENTS

This book is an experiment in the exploration of biblical hermeneutics from a Jungian and archetypal point of view *performed by biblical and theological scholars*. To be sure, the Bible has been the interpretive target of psychologists, and, from time to time, an occasional biblical scholar has made a foray into the field of psychological hermeneutics. But, with the considerable assistance of Trevor Watt and Wayne Rollins, to both of whom the editor is especially indebted, this work constitutes a first organized attempt at a Jungian psychological movement in biblical studies *from the side of biblical scholarship*. Tim Brown and Sandra Hicks also deserve special mention for their research and editorial assistance in the preparation of the manuscript and bibliography.

❈ INTRODUCTION ❈
Psychology, Hermeneutics, and the Bible[1]

WAYNE G. ROLLINS

> We must read our Bible or we shall not understand psychology. Our psychology, whole lives, our language and imagery are built upon the Bible.
>
> C. G. Jung, *The Visions Seminars*[2]

> People will read the gospel again and again and I myself read it again and again. But they will read it with much more profit if they have some insight into their own psyches. Blind are the eyes of anyone who does not know his own heart, and I always recommend the application of a little psychology so that he can understand things like the gospel still better.
>
> C. G. Jung, *Letters*[3]

The Bible is no stranger to Carl Gustav Jung; its words and sentiments travel with Jung literally from cradle to grave. No document is cited by Jung more often, and no cast of characters from any tradition is summoned to the stage of Jung's discourse with greater regularity than the Adam's and Abraham's, the Melchizedek's and Moses', and the Peter's and Paul's of Judaeo-Christian scriptures. No wonder then, that Jung's name is inextricably bound to the new psychological hermeneutic that has emerged at the end of the twentieth century in biblical scholarship.

The present essay will explore Jung's contribution to biblical interpretation under three rubrics: I. Jung and the Emergence of a Biblical-Psychological Hermeneutic; II. The Bible in Jung's Life and Work; and III. Jung's Biblical-Hermeneutical Agenda.

I. JUNG AND THE EMERGENCE OF A BIBLICAL-PSYCHOLOGICAL HERMENEUTIC

"Psychology" has not always enjoyed a favorable press in biblical circles, popular or scholarly. Jung noted a certain, "wrinkling of the nose" among certain clergy at the mention of the word.[4] Biblical scholar Robin Scroggs reports how a discussion of psychological hermeneutics with an older European New Testament scholar in the 1970s ended with the comment, "Bultmann taught us years ago to be suspicious of psychology."[5] Gerd Theissen corroborates Scroggs' experience in the ironic opening line of his *Psychological Aspects of Pauline Theology*: "Every exegete has learned that psychological exegesis is poor exegesis."[6]

The roots of this antipathy to "psychology" in biblical scholarly circles can be traced, in part, to late nineteenth-century reactions to the "psychological interpretation of the person of Jesus" by Karl Hase (1829), Christian Hermann Weisse (1838), and Heinrich Julius Holtzmann (1863), who among others were insisting that a valid historical reconstruction of the life of Jesus must include a "psychological analysis" of his developing messianic self-consciousness. The most enduring blows against these developmental psychological reconstructions were delivered by Albert Schweitzer, who in 1901, denounced them as the products of "mediocre minds which are a patchwork of opinions and apprehend and observe themselves only in a constant flux of development."[7] In 1913 Schweitzer reinforced the attack on "psychology" with the publication of *The Psychiatric Study of Jesus: Exposition and Criticism*, in which he took objection to four medical treatises that had concluded on the basis of psychopathological analysis of the Gospel records that Jesus of Nazareth was "mentally diseased," a conclusion that Schweitzer regarded both on medical and historical-critical grounds as one that should "be rated as exactly zero."[8]

The result within the guild of biblical scholarship was a virtual blackout on things psychological for the better part of a century, from the early 1900s to the 1970s. Mainline biblical scholars routinely dismissed turn of the century works on "biblical psychology," such as Franz Delitzsch's, *A System of Biblical Psychology* (1867), M. Scott Fletcher's, *The Psychology of the New Testament* (1912), and William Sanday's, *Personality in Christ and in Ourselves* (1911).[9] Werner Kümmel's 1972 survey of New

Testament scholarship, *The New Testament: The History of the Investigation of its Problems*, makes no mention of their names or efforts, resorting simply to rehearsing caveats against psychologizing.[10] Occasional friendly flares were sent up, especially by members of the History of Religions school, Hermann Gunkel (1888), Johannes Weiss (1913), and Wilhelm Bousset (1913),[11] and later by Vincent Taylor (1959) and Henry Cadbury (1953),[12] signaling the need to enlist psychological insight in the service of biblical scholarship, but with virtually no response from the field. An occasional scholar such as H. Wheeler Robinson (1946) ignored convention entirely, importing insights from "modern psychology," using the phrase "psychology of inspiration" without apology or explanation.[13] Not until F. C. Grant's essay in 1968, "Psychological Study of the Bible," was a call clearly sounded for a dismantling of the wall that had divided psychology and biblical studies for seven decades, and even then in tones not widely heard.

Two factors account for the change in attitude toward psychology among biblical scholars echoed in Grant's essay. The first is the seismic paradigmatic shift that begins to develop in biblical scholarship in the late 1960s and early 1970s, with the realization that the classical disciplines of historical and literary criticism will no longer prove sufficient in themselves to the increasingly complex and multi-faceted task of biblical interpretation as it is conceived at the end of the twentieth century.[14] John Dominic Crossan observed in 1977, "Biblical study will no longer be conducted under the exclusive or even dominant hegemony" of one or two disciplines, but rather "through a multitude of disciplines interacting mutually as a field criticism."[15] That psychology will be one of those disciplines is indicated in 1991 by the inclusion, for the first time in its history, of a research unit on "Psychology and Biblical Studies" at the annual meeting of the Society of Biblical Literature, the flagship of biblical scholarly associations in the United States. In its 1993 inaugural issue, *Biblical Interpretation: A Journal of Contemporary Approaches* announced the "need for the field of biblical studies to become more public and more pluralistic," inviting the submission of "articles that discuss specific biblical texts in the light of fresh insights that derive from the diversity of relevant disciplines," including sociology, anthropology, archaeology, philosophy, history, linguistics, literary theory, and psychology. Similarly, the Pontifical Biblical Commission in its 1993 document on "The Interpretation of the Bible in the Church" devoted two columns in its survey of contemporary biblical scholarship to "Psychological and Psychoanalytical Approaches" as part of a "methodological spectrum of exegetical work . . . which could not have been envisioned thirty years ago."[16]

A second and primordial factor informing the thaw in the attitude of biblical scholarship toward psychology is the monumental achievement of Sigmund Freud (1856–1939), Carl Jung (1875–1961), and their interpreters. They initiated an entire culture in the art of thinking "psychologically" about itself, its traditions, texts, and institutions.

Freud's contribution to the rapprochement of biblical studies and psychology was indirect. His understanding of the unconscious as the repository of the repressed led Freud to focus on two dimensions of religion: first, its pathological elements, and second, its psychohistorical roots. His critique of religion in *The Future of an Illusion* and his psycho-genetic analyses of religious traditions in *Totem and Taboo* and *Moses and Monotheism* were met initially with resistance in many theological and biblical-critical quarters. Karl Barth characterized his work as "the gruesome morass of the psychology of the unconscious,"[17] and William Foxwell Albright, the dean of biblical archaeological research at the time, alluded to *Moses and Monotheism* as a "futile but widely read example of psychological determinism, . . . totally devoid of serious historical method."[18] These detractors, however, were balanced in time by theological and philosophical proponents, Paul Tillich and Paul Ricoeur among them, who found in Freud penetrating insight into the projective aspect of theological language, neurotic guilt, patterns of infantile wish-fulfillment, the false eschatologization of life that represses present ethical responsibility, and the recurrence of primitive taboos in Judaeo-Christian cultic tales. Although Freud reports autobiographically that an "early preoccupation with the biblical stories, when I had scarcely learned the art of reading, defined in an enduring fashion the direction of my interest,"[19] he did not develop this interest in published form until later in life. He had planned an extended project that would apply psychoanalytic theory to the whole of the Bible, with *Moses and Monotheism* as the initial work,[20] but time ran out.

Accordingly, Freud's legacy for biblical hermeneutics is twofold. First, he lays the groundwork for a psychoanalytic method that can be enlisted to clarify the psychodynamic factors at work in biblical texts, characters, stories, mythic narratives, and religious practices, as scholars such as Francoise Dolto and Gérard Séverin, Carl Healer, Theodor Reik, Richard Rubenstein, Antoine Vergote, and Dorothy Zeligs seek to demonstrate from the professional psychological side, and David Halperin, Dan Merkur, Ilona Rashkow, Richard Rubenstein, Robin Scroggs, Gerd Theissen, Mary Ann Tolbert, and Wilhelm Wuellner from the professional theological and/or biblical-critical side. Second, he advances a hermeneutical *telos*, indigenous to his psychoanalytic goal in general, namely to assist in the achievement of *logos* (reason) and *eros* (love) in the face of *ananke* (necessity="reality").

Jung's contribution to the rapprochement of biblical studies and psychology contrasts with Freud's in several ways. To be sure, Jung stands in Freud's debt. He wrote to physician Edith Schröder in April 1957, "Without Freud's 'psychoanalysis' I would not have had a clue."[21] But as is commonly known, he departed from Freud on matters of fundamental significance that have implications for the application of psychology to biblical hermeneutics. First, Jung views the unconscious, not as a garbage pit of repressed material, but as a creative psychic matrix out of which images, visions, ideas, and dreams can emerge that are compensatory to consciousness in the service of an individuation process both individual and collective in scope. Second, Jung sees religion and all of its expressions and artifacts, not simply as pathological, but as aboriginally and potentiably therapeutic and transformative. Third, and above all for our present purposes, Jung's life and work attest to dependence on, investment in, and commitment to the Bible, its world-picture and world-view, its archetypal images and symbols, and its interpretation in the modern world to a degree unparalleled in the life and work of any twentieth-century psychologist. Freud might have developed his biblical "work" had time not run out. But from beginning to end, Jung's life and work provide congenial and seasoned guidance to the psychologist, theologian, or biblical scholar today who wishes to develop a rationale, methodology, and agenda for the application of psychological insight to the history, text, and interpretation of the Bible. This is evidenced in the work of a number of psychologists and theologians who have applied Jung's thought to biblical interpretation, e.g., Eugen Drewermann, David Cox, Edward Edinger, Joan Chamberlain Engelsman, Peter Homans, Elizabeth Boyden Howes and Sheila Moon of The Guild for Psychological Studies, Joan Chamberlain Engelsman, Morton Kelsey, David L. Miller, Antonio Moreno, John Sanford, Murray Stein, Trevor Watt, and Heinz Westman, as well as of a growing number of biblical scholars (including the present writer), e.g., Schuyler Brown, Adela Yarbro Collins, Maria Kassel, D. Andrew Kille, Diarmuid McGann, Gerd Theissen, Dan Via, Michael E. Willett, Walter Wink, and Wilhelm Wuellner (some of whom contribute to the present volume).

II. THE BIBLE IN JUNG'S LIFE AND WORK

Though the Bible is acknowledged as a factor in Jung's background, it is seldom recognized as a defining reality in the foreground of Jung's life and thought, constituting a major problem and project Jung addresses throughout his career. Raised in a Swiss Reformed Protestant parsonage and engaged as a youth in active dialogue with six clergy on his mother's side and two clergy uncles on his father's, Jung was initiated into a lifelong relationship and dialogue with the Bible. He writes in a 1957 letter, "You can rest assured that having studied the Gospels for a life-time (I am nearly 83!) I am pretty well acquainted with the foundations of our Christianity."[22] But it was precisely this nineteenth-century biblical context in tension with Jung's emerging thought and experience that framed the problem and provided the point of departure for the lifelong project that the Bible would constitute for him both at the conscious and unconscious level, providing guidelines for a biblical-psychological hermeneutical agenda today.

A. *The Bible as Problem and Project for Jung.* The problem that the Bible presents for Jung can be seen in a series of four feeling-toned experiences and associations in which it becomes evident that the problem of the Bible in Western culture and its proper understanding and interpretation will become a major item in Jung's personal and progressional agenda and will generate an autonomous complex that manifests itself both at conscious and unconscious levels in his life and work.

The first of these feeling-toned associations is the Biblicism of the Reformed Protestant piety and theology that Jung recalls vividly from his youth. The theological language of Reformed Protestantism seemed unrelated to experience, and as a child he found it "stale and hollow, like a tale told by someone who knows it only by hearsay and cannot quite believe it in himself."[23] "So long as religion is only faith and outward form, and the religious function is not experienced in our own souls," Jung writes, "nothing of any importance has happened. It has yet to be understood that the *mysterium magnum* is not only an actuality but is first and foremost rooted in the human psyche."[24] Jung found it too often to be the case that "the Christian puts his Church and his Bible between himself and his unconscious,"[25] on the one hand rehearsing dogmatic formulae without thinking, and on the other, suppressing awareness of the "God within" of which Jung had read in Paul, John, and the mystics. Such types of religion seemed to Jung to be "more interested in protecting their institutions than in understanding the mystery that symbols present," having "stripped all things of their mystery and numinosity."[26] Jung observes furthermore that "such a religion . . . is incapable of giving help and having any other moral effect."[27] Jung came to the conclusion,"Why, that is not religion at all."[28]

A second feeling-toned association that informs Jung's biblical "complex" is his assessment of the historical-biblical critical scholarship that proceeds from what Jung calls "the garish conceits of enlightenment.[29] Jung found this type of "rationalistic historicism" guilty of excising the numinous aspect from the Bible, severing it from "the living religious process,"[30] and defusing its powerful symbols and stories through "demythologization."[31] In his Terry lectures at Yale, Jung wrote: "Nor has scientific criticism . . . been very helpful in enhancing belief in the divine character of the holy scriptures. It is also a fact that under the influence of a so-called scientific enlightenment great masses of educated people have either left the church or have become profoundly indifferent to it. If they were all dull rationalists or neurotic intellectuals, the loss would not be regrettable. But many of them are religious people. . . ."[32]

This is not to say that Jung was ignorant of or opposed to biblical scholarship; quite the contrary, as demonstrated in a letter to American writer, Upton Sinclair, who had written for Jung's opinion on his new novel, *A Personal Jesus.* Jung's response demonstrates his familiarity with biblical Greek, ancient near Eastern literature, and the recent history of biblical scholarship. Recalling the "Life of Jesus research" of Ernest Renan, David Strauss, and Albert Schweitzer, Jung criticizes Sinclair for excluding certain portions of the text as "later interpolations," in order to create a portrait of Jesus "convincing to a modern American mind." "You give an excellent picture of a possible religious teacher," he writes Sinclair, "But you give us no understanding of what the New Testament tries to tell, namely the life, fate, and effect of a God-Man. . . ." Jung concludes with the injunction, "Sure enough, we must believe in Reason. But it should not prevent us from recognizing a mystery when we meet one. It seems to me that no rational biography could explain one of the most 'irrational' effects ever observed in the history of man. I believe that this problem can only be approached through history and comparative psychology of symbols."[33] Jung states that his critical approach to the Bible is more akin to that of Wilhelm de Wette (1780–1849), founder of the historical critical approach to the Pentateuch and friend of Jung's grandfather, whose hermeneutical method was to "mythize" or extract the "symbolic value" of "marvelous" Bible stories.[34]

A third feeling-laden association, directly related to the previous two, is the tragedy of Jung's Pastor father, Johann Paul Achilles Jung, who died when Carl was 21, caught between the desire to remain loyal to the unquestioning "faith" of the biblical piety to which he had been ordained, and, one suspects, the "rationalistic historicism" of Enlightenment biblical scholarship that fed the "doubt" he so much feared.[35] "It was the tragedy of my youth," Jung writes, "to see my father cracking up before my eyes on the problem of his faith and dying an early death."[36]

Jung had been told by his father at an early age, "You always want to think. One ought not to think, but believe."[37] Years later Jung wrote that "people who merely believe and don't think always forget that they continually expose themselves to their own worst enemy: doubt. Wherever belief reigns, doubt lurks in the background."[38] Jung saw this belief-doubt scenario play itself out in the years preceding the death of his father, who had become increasingly lonely, irritable, and hypochondriac. "Once I heard him praying," Jung reports. "He struggled desperately to keep his faith. I was shaken and outraged at once, because I saw how hopelessly he was entrapped by the Church and its theological thinking. They had blocked all avenues by which he might have reached God directly, and then faithlessly abandoned him."[39]

The tragedy was heightened by the fact that Jung's father had once had an active intellectual life. He "had studied Oriental languages in Göttingen and done his dissertation on the Arabic version of the Song of Songs."[40] As a minister he had been "connected with the cantonal insane asylum" and was "very much interested in psychiatry," a fact that had ironically inclined Jung at first in the opposite direction.[41] Shortly before his death he had also begun reading in Bernheim's book on suggestion in Sigmund Freud's translation. But none of this had succeeded in enabling his father to rise above the "sentimental idealism" of the "country parson, smoking a long student's pipe, . . . reading novels or an occasional travel book."[42]

Not only had Jung's father made the *sacrificium intellectus* in his attitude toward the Bible and religion, he had also failed to discover what the prophets, Paul, and the young Jung had come to know, namely that the promptings of the "inner man" or the "God within" are to be accorded as much authority as the voice of traditional religion.[43] In Jung's words, his father "had taken the Bible's commandments as his guide; he believed in God as the Bible prescribed and as his forefathers had taught him. But he did not know the immediate living God who stands, omnipotent and free, above His Bible and His Church, who calls upon man to partake of His freedom, and can force him to renounce his own views and convictions in order to fulfill without reserve the command of God."[44]

In the end Jung tells us, surprisingly, that his father's tragic death did not forestall Jung's interest in religion, but provided the "objective outer event that opened my eyes to the importance of religion" despite all the "negative conclusions" about religion that might have seemed warranted.[45] Jung saw his father's tragedy as a mantle of unfinished business he was destined to assume. He writes, "I feel very strongly that I am under the influence of things or questions which were left incomplete and unanswered by my parents and grandparents and more distant ancestors . . . It has always seemed to me that I had to answer questions which fate had posed to my forefathers, and which had not yet been answered, or as if I had to complete, or perhaps continue, things which previous ages had left unfinished."[46] His father's death marked the beginning of a project for Jung, vindicating his father's life, his father's religion, and his father's commitment to the Bible, albeit from a "psychological" perspective that his father at best was only beginning to understand.

A final feeling-toned association Jung has with the Bible has to do with Jung's personal acknowledgement of the significance of biblical archetypal images for his own life, as well as for Western culture in general. One example of the former, from among many, is his recounting how the image of Paul came to his rescue at the time of his father's death, when by all accounts, he should have thrown in the towel on religion, but didn't, and in fact went on to develop his psychology:

> My education offered me nothing but arguments against religion on the one hand, and on the other the charisma of faith was denied me. I was thrown back on experience alone. Always Paul's experience on the road to Damascus hovered before me, and I asked myself how his fate would have fallen out but for his visions. Yet this experience came upon him while he was blindly pursuing his own way. As a young man I drew the conclusion that you must obviously fulfill your destiny in order to get to the point where a *donum gratiae* might happen along. But I was far from certain, and always kept the possibility in mind that on this road I might end up in a black hole. I have remained true to this attitude all my life. From this you can easily see the origin of my psychology: only by going my own way, integrating my capacities headlong (like Paul), and thus creating a foundation for myself, could something be vouchsafed to me or built upon it, no matter where it came from, and of which I could be reasonably sure that it was not merely one of my own neglected capacities.[47]

An example of the latter, i.e., Jung's sense of the cultural impact of the Bible, is voiced in the text of Jung's *Visions Seminar* (1930–34): "We must read the Bible or we shall not understand psychology. Our psychology, whole lives, our language and imagery are built upon the Bible."[48] On the basis of this dictum and the many feeling-toned associations Jung has with the Bible and the problems of its meaning and interpretation, it comes as no surprise that the Bible constitutes a project of major significance in Jung's life and work, both at the conscious and unconscious level.

B. The Bible as Conscious Project in Jung's Life and Work.
Although the ubiquity of the Bible in Jung's life and work is a
matter of public record, it is seldom acknowledged by Jungian
commentators or biographers. For example, Vincent Brome's
Jung: Man and Myth includes an appendix on "Jung's Sources," in
which he cites philosophers, psychologists,novelists, poets, and
history of religions texts—from Plato, to Freud, to Rider Haggard,
Goethe, and the Tibetan Book of the Dead. Not once does Brome
mention the Bible, the single text that is cited more often than any
other document in the Jungian corpus. To set the record straight
we will examine four moments in Jung's *curriculum vitae* that
make his conscious and comprehensive use of the Bible mani-
festly evident.

The first example comes from Jung's medical student days, in
January, 1899. Jung was twenty-four years old and was taking
his turn as lecturer for the "Basel section of the colorwearing
Zofingia" society that he had joined four years earlier, and to
which his father had belonged in his student days.[49] The lecture
title was unlikely for a medical student: "Thoughts on the
Interpretation of Christianity, with Reference to the Theory of
Albrecht Ritschl."[50] Ritschl (1822–89) was a systematic theologian
to whose thought Jung had recently been introduced (by his
father's former vicar) as one of the "new aspects of Protestant theology . . . much in fashion in those days." Jung found the "historicism" of Ritschl's theology "irritating,"[51] and in his lecture flew
into Ritschl's anti-mystical interpretation of Christian origins. The
remarkable feature of the lecture from our standpoint is the list of
fifty-five numbered biblical passages (e.g., Matt. 13:35, "I will open
my mouth in parables; I will utter things which have been kept
secret from the foundation of the world;" or Luke 12:49, "I am
come to send fire on the earth") that Jung had mustered for the
disquisition, demonstrating a practice that would mark Jung's
career of enlisting biblical wisdom to combat mindless pietism and
rationalistic positivism.

A second example of the nuclear role of the Bible in Jung's life
is his *Answer to Job* (1951), the single essay he addresses explicitly to a biblical theme (one that qualifies as an unconscious project as well as a conscious one in Jung's life and work). According
to Jungian analyst Nathan Schwartz-Salant, Jung found *Answer*

to Job the only work of his he found "totally satisfying."[52] He wrote
to Henry Corbin: "the Book 'came to me' . . . as if accompanied by
the great music of a Bach or Handel."[53] In a letter to Aniela Jaffé
in May, 1951, he states: "In this way I have landed the great
whale; I mean 'Answer to Job.' I can't say I have fully digested this
tour de force of the unconscious." Later in July he writes, "If there
is anything like the spirit seizing one by the scruff of the neck, it
was the way this book came into being."[54] In the "Lectori
Benevolo" of the essay he adverts to the level of feeling and the
depth of emotion that the subject matter touches in him. "Since I
shall be dealing with numinous factors, my feeling is challenged
quite as much as my intellect. I cannot, therefore, write in a coolly
objective manner, but must allow my emotional subjectivity to
speak if I want to describe what I feel when I read certain books of
the Bible, or when I remember the impressions I have received
from the doctrines of our faith. . . . What I am expressing is first of
all my own personal view, but I know that I also speak in the
name of many who have had similar experiences."[55]

Answer to Job is the product of a long-term agenda for Jung,
things he says "I have been occupied with . . . for years."[56] He had
hesitated for many years to undertake the book, knowing its publication would cause fierce controversy. It occasioned a rift with
long-time theologian friend, Victor White—"even Emma Jung had
misgivings," as Wehr has observed.[57] Jung proceeded, however,
because of his compulsion "to write down from the heart everything that had formed an indelible part of his life for decades."[58]
Answer to Job is a reprise of the great themes and problems with
which Jung had wrestled from the beginning. As Answer to Job
speaks of Job's expecting "help from God against God," it also
reveals Jung expecting help from the Bible (and psychology)
against the Bible as misunderstood by the Biblicistic piety and
rationalistic biblical criticism that Jung had so profoundly
opposed.

Another subtle dimension of the importance of Answer to Job
for Jung's personal life is that it provided a parabolic analogue
and antidote to the tragic route his father's life had assumed.
Jung intimates this in his autobiography, speaking of his father:
"He had to quarrel with somebody, so he did it with his family
and himself. Why didn't he do it with God, the dark author of all

created things, who alone was responsible for the sufferings of the world? God would assuredly have sent him by way of an answer one of those magical, infinitely profound dreams which He had sent to me even without being asked, and which had sealed my fate."[59]

A third genre of evidence for the role the Bible plays as conscious project in Jung's life and work is the testimony of the twenty volumes of the *Collected Works*, which lists twenty columns in its General Index under the entry, "Bible," exceeding the number of columns devoted to any other single text.[60] The listing includes reference to all but thirteen of the sixty-six books of the Old and New Testaments of the Christian canon, as well as to Old Testament Apocryphal and pseudepigraphic writings (Life of Adam and Eve, Syrian Apocalypse of Baruch, Ecclesiasticus, Book of Enoch, II Esdras, Tobit, and Wisdom of Solomon) and from New Testament apocryphal works (Book of Apostle Bartholomew, Gospel of the Egyptians, *Epistolae Apostolorum*, Ascension of Isaiah, Acts of John, Acts of Peter, Gospel of Peter, Gospel of Philip, Apocalypse of Zephaniah, and Acts of Thomas), along with references to the critical volumes by R. H. Charles on the Apocrypha and Pseudepigrapha of the Old Testament and on the works on the New Testament apocrypha by Edgar Hennecke and by M. R. James.

Beyond the enclave of twenty columns indexing the "Bible" is a vast network of separate headings for biblical names, terms, stories, themes, and phrases, along with references to theologians and biblical interpreters. Proceeding through the *General Index* from "A" to "Z" one finds 185 biblical names, many cited more than a dozen times. For example, the entries under the letter "A" include the personal names Aaron, Abel, Abraham, Adah (wife of Esau), Adoni-Bezek (a Canaanite king), Ahasuerus, Ahijah, Andrew, Azazel (the scapegoat), and Augustus. In addition to the personal names are biblical topics and themes, e.g., abyss, Amorites, Antichrist, Annunciation, Antiochus, Apostle, Ark of the Covenant, Areopagus, Ascension, along with terms in Greek script, *anthropos* (man) and *agnoia* (ignorance), and the Latin phrase *agnata fides* (consanguine faith), and the Hebrew *adamah* (earth), *aleph* and *tau* (= "A and Z"). It also includes ancient writers and biblical commentators (Abelard, Albertus Magnus, Ambrose, Anselm, and Augustine). At the other end of the alphabet, the letter "Z" yields an appreciably shorter list, including Zecharias, Mt. Zion, Zipporah (wife of Moses), and Zohar. Running through the alphabet between "A" and "Z" is a panoply of biblical entities, including, Balaam, the Canaanites, Dagon the God of the Philistines, El Elyon (God most High), the flood, Gamaliel, Hagar, Immanuel, Jezebel, the Kingdom of God, Lilith, Melchisedek, Nicodemus, the "only-begotten," the Paraclete, Queen of Sheba, Rahab, the Shulamite Woman, Terah (father of Abraham), the "unjust steward," the *vox dei*, the whirlwind, and Yehoshua.

In addition to this glossary of biblical names is a compendium of 230 biblical terms, phrases, and themes, e.g., the "inner man," central to Jung's anthropology; the "mote in your brother's eye," which Jung adduces as an illustration of projection; and the Christological question, "Why callest Thou me good?" which Jung often summons to demonstrate the humanity of Jesus in the Gospels. Repeatedly Jung finds that the Bible supplies him with archetypal images that inform his situation: the pearl of great price, the house built on sand, the grain of mustard seed, the journey of Adam out of the garden, and the buried treasure in the field.

A letter of Jung's from March 13, 1958, aptly demonstrates his perennially artful interpolation of biblical images (indicated by italics below) that articulate ideas central to his self-understanding:

> The primordial experience is not concerned with the historical bases of Christianity but consists in an immediate experience of God (as was had by *Moses, Job, Hosea, Ezekiel* among others) which "con-vinces" because it is "overpowering." But this is something you can't easily talk about. One can only say that somehow one has to reach the rim of the world or get to the end of one's tether in order to partake of the terror or grace of such an experience at all. Its nature is such that it is really understandable why the Church is actually a place of refuge or protection for those who cannot endure the fire of the divine presence. *A logion says: "He that is near me is near the fire. He that is far from me is far from the kingdom."* I think I understand ecclesiastical Christianity but the theologians do not understand me. Their *raison d'être* consists in the very fact of belonging to a Church, and mine in coming to terms with that indefinable being we call "God." Probably no compromise is possible except that of "coexistence," each allowing the other his say. At any rate, again and again the allegory is repeated of the *strait and steep path trodden by the few and the broad path trodden by the many*. . . .[61]

A fourth and final demonstration of the Bible as conscious project for Jung is the vertical marker in the family graveyard plot at Küsnacht that contains the family crest and, on the side, two Latin inscriptions. The first is, "Vocatus atque non vocatus, Deus aderit" (Summoned or not summoned God will be present), the oracular Delphic utterance Jung found in Erasmus that he had also inscribed over the entranceway at Küsnacht for his patients. The second is the citation of I Cor. 15:47, "Primus homo terrenus de terra, secundus homo coelestis de coelo" (The first man is of the earth, a man of dust: the second is of heaven). The Bible is part of Jung's conscious project from beginning to end.

C. *The Bible as Unconscious Project in Jung's Life and Work.* One would expect from the above that the Bible might seep into Jung's dream life, as it did on a number of occasions documented by Jung. The first occurred, in December, 1913, at the onset of the four-year period when Jung made his descent into the unconscious to document images that appear spontaneously in the psyche, using himself as a case study. He recounts a dream in which two, and possibly three, biblical figures, appear—an old man with a white beard who identified himself as Elijah and a young, beautiful, blind girl named Salome, in the company of a black serpent which, Jung reports, "displayed an unmistakable fondness for me. I stuck close to Elijah because he seemed to be the most reasonable of the three, and to have a clear intelligence. Of Salome I was distinctly suspicious. Elijah and I had a long conversation which, however, I did not understand." Jung comments, "Naturally I tried to find a plausible explanation for the appearance of biblical figures in my fantasy by reminding myself that my father had been a clergyman. But that really explained nothing at all."[62] Jung was later to identify the black serpent as symbolizing the "introverting libido," Salome, the anima, and Elijah, the Mahatma, the Wise old Man (1989: 88–90, 92–99).[63] Jung cited the dream as an example of the spontaneous manifestation of mythic themes in biblical guise, though made no further speculation on why his unconscious chose biblical imagery to express the archetype, rather than some other symbolic vocabulary.

Jung reports a second, and for our purposes, more significant dream in which the Bible and his father are paired in key roles related to Jung's preoccupation with the issues addressed in *Answer to Job*.[64] Jung writes, "The problem of Job in all of its ramifications had likewise been foreshadowed in a dream. It started with my paying a visit to my long-deceased father, "who in the dream is not only the guardian of the sarcophagi of famous people at a large eighteenth-century home, but also a "distinguished scholar in his own right." In the dream Jung meets his father in the study, where "oddly enough, Dr. Y.—who was about my age—and his son, both psychiatrists, were also present." To illustrate a point in the conversation, Jung's father "fetched a big Bible down from a shelf . . . bound in shiny fish-skin," opened it to the Pentateuch, "and began interpreting a certain passage." Jung recounts that "he did this so swiftly and so learnedly that I could not follow him. I noted only that what he said betrayed a vast amount of variegated knowledge. . . . I saw that Dr. Y. understood nothing at all, and his son began to laugh. They thought that my father was going off the deep end and what he said was simply senile prattle. But it was quite clear to me . . . that there was nothing silly about what he was saying. On the contrary, his argument was so intelligent and so learned that we in our stupidity simply could not follow it. It dealt with something extremely important which fascinated him . . . his mind was flooded with profound ideas. I was annoyed and thought it was a pity that he had to talk in the presence of three such idiots as we."[65]

Jung's comment on the dream identifies the two psychiatrists, Dr. Y. and his son, as representations of the "limited medical point of view" that had in fact infected Jung's own thinking. The rest of the scene, for Jung, pointed to the unconscious task that he was to undertake in the writing of Job, that he had left to his "'father,' that is, to the unconscious." Jung comments that in the dream, his father "was obviously engrossed in the Bible (Genesis?) and eager to communicate his insights. The fishskin marks the Bible as an unconscious content, for fishes are mute and unconscious. My poor father does not succeed in communicating either." In connection with a later scene in the dream Jung adds, "something in me was defiant and determined not to be a dumb fish: and," he adds, "if there were not something of the sort in free men, no Book of Job would have been written several hundred years before the birth of Christ."[66]

A second dream that Jung reports as prelude to *Answer to Job* begins with Jung in his own house discovering a "large wing which I had never visited. . . . When I opened it, I found myself in a room set up as a laboratory. . . . This was my father's workroom. However, he was not there. On shelves along the walls stood hundreds of bottles containing every imaginable sort of fish. I was astonished: so now my father was going in for ichthyology!"[67] Jung interprets the fish (*ichthys*) as a clear reference to his "preoccupation with Christ, and finds it "remarkable" that the study of fish was attributed to his father. Jung's dream saw his father as a "caretaker of Christian souls" (as his mother also was in a second part of the dream). For Jung the dream signified the contiguity of his vocational task with that of his parents. He writes, "Both my parents appeared burdened with the problem of the 'cure of souls,' which in fact was really my task. Something had remained unfinished and was still with my parents; that is to say, it was still later in the unconscious and hence reserved for the future."[68]

Jung discloses that "all problems that concerned me personally or scientifically" were "accompanied or heralded by dreams."[69] In response to the two dreams Jung undertakes the daunting but compelling task of *Answer to Job*, bringing together his lifelong wrestling with religion and the Bible in the service of the "many questions from the public and from patients. . . about the religious problems of modern man"[70] which for Jung included the question of biblical hermeneutics. In so doing, Jung hoped to point the way to a solution of the problems on which his father had tragically foundered. Jung writes, "He wanted to rest content with faith, but faith broke faith with him. Such is frequently the reward for the *sacrificium intellectus*. . . . Blind acceptance never leads to a solution; at best it leads only to a standstill and is paid for heavily in the next generation."[71] It was Jung's commission, from the voice of his unconscious, to offset the debt of his father's irresolution, by reclaiming the meaning that his father had failed to detect in Scripture as well as in the recesses of his own psyche, toward the final goal of the "cure of souls."

III. JUNG'S BIBLICAL-HERMENEUTICAL AGENDA

Jung's long-term agenda for the Bible is subsumed under his agenda for the Christian tradition in general. As Murray Stein has so skillfully argued in *Jung's Treatment of Christianity: The Psychotherapy of a Religious Tradition*, Jung's approach to Christianity is not primarily that of the "empirical scientist" who wishes to lay bare the psychological anatomy of religion, nor of the "hermeneutical revivalist" who wishes to reclaim the lost meaning of Christian symbolism, nor of the "doctor of souls" who seeks to heal those wounded by religion, nor of the "Post-Christian modern man" who sifts through the detritus of Christianity to repudiate the bad and assimilate the good. Jung's approach is that of a psychotherapist, with the "strong urge to heal Christianity."[72] Or as James Dittes frames it, Jung's objective is that of "a prophet or reformer wanting to rescue the best of his tradition from the worst of his tradition," calling for it "to grow beyond a one-sidedness in which it is stuck . . . and beyond paralyzing literalisms, rationalisms, and perfectionisms that dangerously remove religion from its origins and mission in experience." In the end "he wants Christianity, as he must have wanted his father and mother, to become transformed, liberated, renewing its vitality in restored connection with the roots from which it arose."[73]

What hermeneutical program does Jung advance to achieve this objective with the Bible? As Peter Homans observes in his essay, "Psychology and Hermeneutics: Jung's Contribution," Jung does not provide a full-blown hermeneutical system nor does he delineate "the full range of problems involved in a theory of interpretation of religious forms."[74] But the Jungian corpus does leave two resources for attempting the construction of a Jungian hermeneutical model. The first is a scattering of essays in which Jung addresses the problem of the hermeneutics of literature and art directly, e.g., *Answer to Job* (*CW* 11), "Commentary on 'The Secret of the Golden Flower'" (*CW* 13), "On the Relation of Analytical Psychology to Poetry" (*CW* 15), and above all, "Psychology and Literature" (*CW* 15). The second is the myriad of interpretive comments Jung makes on biblical texts throughout the Jungian corpus. From these two sources, one can extract a number of hermeneutical presuppositions, an agenda of hermeneutical objectives, and a hermeneutical method for a psychological approach to the Bible.

A. *Presuppositions for a Jungian Psycho-Hermeneutical Approach to the Bible.* The first and fundamental presupposition for a Jungian hermeneutic is that religion and religious texts are "not only a sociological and historical phenomenon" but also a function of the "psychological structure of human personality."[75] As Jung notes in the introduction to his essay on "Psychology and Literature," although poetry "constitutes the proper province of literary science and of aesthetics . . . it is also a psychic phenomenon, and as such it probably must be taken into account by the psychologist."[76] For Jung "the human psyche is the womb of all the arts and sciences,"[77] which means that all human expression, including religion, art, and literature have been processed through the human psyche and can be shown to bear evidence of the psychic habits, processes, dispositions, truths, and visions that gave birth to them. His goal therefore is to "discover psychological facts and processes that before were veiled in symbols and beyond . . . comprehension."[78]

It should be noted that Jung is eager to distance his "psychological approach" from the "psychologizing" approach he identifies with Freud, which tends to use psychological analysis to reduce a psychic artifact (e.g., a poem, work of art, piece of literature, an image of God, or a dogma) either to an illusion or to a symptom of neurosis. The result of this approach in the popular mind, Jung claims, has been that "every attempt at adequate psychological understanding is immediately suspected of psychologism."[79] Jung argues that this need not be the case if psychological inquiry focuses on the content of symbolic expression[80] rather than on the psychological state of the author. "The personal life of the artist is at most a help or a hindrance, but is never essential to his creative task, . . . his personal career may be interesting and inevitable, but it does not explain his art. . . . The essence of a work of art is not to be bound in the personal idiosyncrasies that creep into it . . . but in its rising above the personal and speaking from the mind and heart of the artists to the mind and heart of mankind."[81]

A second psychological presupposition of a Jungian psycho-hermeneutical approach, implicit in the first, is the recognition of the unconscious as a factor ineluctably at work in all human expression, including religious texts. Jung identifies three aspects of the unconscious at work in religious texts worthy of reflection as part of a psychological hermeneutic.

The first consists of the remnants of the pre-Christian or pre-Israelite consciousness that reside unconsciously in

Christian and Hebrew sacred texts. Speaking of Christianity specifically, Jung writes, "Everything has its history, everything has 'grown,' and Christianity, which is supposed to have appeared suddenly as a unique revelation from heaven, undoubtedly also has its history. . . . It is exactly as if we had built a cathedral over a pagan temple and no longer knew that it is still there underneath." Jung adds that the presence of pre-Christian factors in Christian texts, unconscious as they are, continue to have their effect, and that as contemporary Western culture has the unconscious stamp of Judaeo-Christianity upon it, so "we are also stamped by what existed before Christianity."[82]

A second unconscious factor at work in religious texts worthy of psycho-hermeneutical attention is the personal unconscious of the author of the text. Jung, to be sure, is wary of focusing on the author or artist more than the final text, as noted above, and insists that although "the personal psychology of the artist may explain many aspects of his work," it does not explain "the work itself."[83] Be that as it may, a psychological approach from a Jungian perspective will assume two primary factors in the personal unconscious of the author at work in the text: (a) the psychological-type orientation of the writer (sensing, thinking, feeling, intuiting), which will manifest itself in the treatment and choice of materials in the text; and (b) the psychological history of the author, the complexes, projections, sublimations, urges, passions, etc. that will be at work in the warp and woof of the text as a psycho-hermeneutical factor, difficult to identify with any degree of accuracy to be sure, but nonetheless present as a psycho-hermeneutical fact.

A third unconscious factor at work in religious texts, of consummate interest to Jung, is the collective unconscious, or as Jung also alludes to it, the objective unconscious, which Jung describes as "a sphere of unconscious mythology whose primordial images are the common heritage of mankind."[84] Though the objective unconscious "will forever elude our attempts at understanding,"[85] its traces can be detected in many genres of scriptural expression (e.g., symbols, archetypal images, dream narratives, stories, myths, epic narratives, apocalypses, stories of heroic figures). The contemplation and amplification of such images constitutes a major part of a psycho-hermeneutical agenda, examining their function and effect in the biblical text and in Bible-reading communities, comparing their form and content with commensurate images in other cultural traditions, and inquiring into their meaning for the human condition.

B. An Agenda for a Jungian Psycho-Hermeneutical Approach to the Bible. With this set of presuppositions about the text implicit in a psycho-hermeneutical approach to the Bible, let us proceed to an eight-point agenda that would seem to be inferred in the Jungian corpus for the application of a "psychological approach" to the text.

1. Symbols, archetypal images, and myths constitute the most obvious and primary point of inquiry for a Jungian psycho-hermeneutic, since, as noted above, they seem to be the primary point of access to the great themes indigenous to the collective unconscious. A keystone of Jung's psychology is first, that the unconscious spontaneously produces images of direction and integration for the individual and culture, and second, that classical religions traffic in such images, which in the end have to do, not just with history "back then" or "out there" but with the "now" and the "within." In a letter to Dorothee Hoch on July 3, 1952, Jung wrote: "Educated people . . . would be much more readily convinced of the meaning of the gospel if it were shown them the myth was always there to a greater or lesser degree, and moreover is actually present in archetypal form in every individual. Then people would understand where, in spite of its having been artificially screened off by the theologians, the gospel really touches them and what it is talking about."[86]

The purpose of symbols, archetypal images, and myths within the economy of the psyche from Jung's perspective is to correct the "course" of the psyche when it has become "one-sided or adopts a false attitude."[87] This will occur not only as a corrective to an individual psyche, but to the psychic attitude of an entire culture or age when it becomes side-tracked or when it forgets its *raison d'être*. The medium of psychic expression in the case of the individual is often the dream, but in the case of an entire culture it may be a "dream" mediated through great literature, music, or art. "Herein lies the social significance of art," Jung writes. "It is constantly at work educating the spirit of the age, conjuring up the forms in which the age is most lacking. The unsatisfied yearning of the artist reaches back to the primordial image in the unconscious which is best fitted to compensate the inadequacy and one-sidedness of the present." More often than not, the artist of which Jung speaks bears social resemblance to the Old Testament prophets, by virtue of their lack of adaptation to their culture around them which provides them with the eyes to see "the psychic elements that are waiting to play their part in the life of the collective." In this instance, Jung writes, "the lack of adaptation turns out to his advantage" and to that of the collective psyche.[88]

How is one to approach these spontaneous and compensatory images mediated through symbol, archetypal image, and myth? Here the profound difference between Freud's hermeneutic and Jung's becomes clear. Jung contends that for Freud, symbols "are not true symbols" but "*signs* or *symptoms* of the subliminal [repressive] processes." He continues:

> The true symbol differs essentially from this, and should be understood as an expression of an intuitive idea that cannot yet be formulated in any other or better way. When Plato, for instance, puts the whole problem of the theory of knowledge in his parable of the cave, or when Christ expresses the idea of the Kingdom of Heaven in parables, these are genuine and true symbols, that is, attempts to express something for which no verbal concept yet exists. If we were to interpret Plato's metaphor in Freudian terms we would naturally arrive at the uterus and would have proved that even a mind like Plato's was still stuck on a primitive level of infantile sexuality. But we would have completely overlooked what Plato actually created . . . ; we would have missed the essential point. . . .[89]

A Jungian hermeneutical approach to symbols, archetypal images, and myths, therefore challenges the reader not only to understand the manifest content of the story, fable, parable, or image in its own linguistic and cultural setting, but to contemplate the image toward the end of finding "our way back to the deepest springs of life" that the artist, poet, or storyteller has crystallized with imaginal rendering.[90] This will not be a matter of a simple, univocal translation, but an exercise in entertaining the paradoxical amplitude of the image in which "fullness of life" and the "incomprehensible" are expressed in forms that eschew the onesidedness of "non-ambiguity and non-contradiction."[91]

Two of the essays in the present volume seek to demonstrate this aspect of a Jungian hermeneutic: Schuyler Brown's exploration of the history and meaning of "The Myth of Sophia" and Michael Willett Newheart's critical analysis, "Johannine Symbolism." These point the way to further research, not only into the vast sea of biblical images, but in the transmutations they have undergone in the theological forms and dogmas of the developing tradition.

2. Dreams constitute a second, specialized focus for a Jungian psycho-hermeneutic of the Bible. Although Sigmund Freud provided the "royal road" to modern dream interpretation, C. G. Jung developed the oneirocritical theory that provided access to biblical dreams and dream interpretation from a perspective congenial to a biblical view of dreams. Freud's psychopathological approach, which regarded the dream as an intentionally disguised expression of repressed instinctual urges that should be dredged into consciousness, focused not on the dream itself but on its latent content, using a method of "free association" to tease out that content for conscious recognition, in effect regarding the dream as a mask for a darker, repressed reality. Jung's theory, on the other hand saw the dream in biblically-compatible terms as part of the self-regulating system of the psyche which provided images compensatory to and therapeutic for consciousness (Job 33:15–17). As a result, the role, meaning, and significance of biblical dreams has become a subject for critical examination from a biblical-critical and Jungian perspective, with pioneer work done by Morton Kelsey in his invaluable history of dream interpretation, *Dreams: The Dark Speech of the Spirit* and by John Sanford in *Dreams: God's Forgotten Language.*

A Jungian psycho-hermeneutic approach can make a number of contributions to the study of biblical dreams, though at the outset it should be noted that Jungian dream theory would preclude the possibility of interpreting a biblical dream from the standpoint of a biblical dreamer, giving the unavailability of the dreamer for comment. Beyond this obvious caveat, a psycho-hermeneutical approach can contribute to the work of biblical exegesis in at least four ways. First, it can offer a classification of a given biblical dream from the standpoint of a Jungian typology of dreams (e.g initial dreams, "big dreams," recurrent dreams), locating the biblical dream in the broader context of human dreaming in general. Second, it can contribute to a history of dream interpretation, comparing the oneiro-interpretive approach of the Bible with that of Greco-Roman culture, Rabbinic Judaism, and later Christian writers, e.g., Clement, John Chrysostom, and Augustine. Third, it can provide insight into the legitimacy of the oneirointerpretive approach of the biblical writers in their reporting of dreams, and of the dream interpretations proffered by figures within the biblical narrative, e.g., Peter's recurrent "universalistic" dream and its interpretation in Acts 10:9–16. Fourth, it can provide possible insight into the archetypal dimensions of certain dream images in the Bible as applicable species-wide. In the present volume, these are among the considerations offered in Trevor Watt's essay on "Joseph's Dreams."

3. Biblical personalities constitute a third subject on which a psycho-hermeneutic approach can cast light. As has been demonstrated in John Sanford's studies of the biblical portraits of Jacob, Joseph, Moses, Adam and Eve, and Saul, "the tragic hero," and in Edward Edinger's studies on Abraham, Jacob, Moses, Joshua, Gideon, Samson, Ruth, Saul, David, Solomon, Old Testament prophets and kings, in Walter Wink's essay on Jacob's wrestling with God, or in André and Pierre-Emmanuel LaCocque's study of Jonah, a psycho-hermeneutic approach to biblical personalities offers two, and possibly three, new lines of inquiry and exegesis to the study of the text. The first is simply character analysis from a psychological perspective, analyzing the psychic habits, strategies, and defenses implicit in the textual portrait of a biblical figure, commenting, albeit tentatively, on the conscious as well as unconscious factors and intentions that appear to be operative within the psycho-dynamics of the narrative. Such analysis will add a psychological dimension to the rich interpretive work being done by the new literary and narrative criticism.

A second line of inquiry focuses on the biblical portraits' personalities as models of individuation, consciously or unconsciously intended by the biblical author. Jung enjoins us "to examine carefully the psychological aspects of the individuation process in the light of Christian tradition, which can describe it for us with an exactness and impressiveness far surpassing our feeble attempts,"[92] and he explicitly identifies such models of individuation in the biblical figures of Adam, Abraham, Paul, and preeminently of Christ as the exemplification of the archetype of the Self. Such analysis would assist the biblical scholar not only in adding a psychological dimension to current rhetorical criticism,[93] which seeks to detect the "purpose" and motivation of a text (which in this case would be to communicate a model of individuation), but will reinforce the Jungian hermeneutical objective of showing how the text relates to life. The article in the present volume by D. Andrew Kille, "Jacob—A Study in Individuation," provides a paradigm for research in this area.

A third possible contribution of a psychological approach to biblical personalities is psychoanalytic. Though Jung in his time objected strongly to the Freudian focus on the psychopathology of biblical authors, it cannot be gainsaid that psychoanalytic observations on biblical portraits of personalities can be of value to the biblical interpreter. Though a psychoanalysis of biblical figures in the strictest sense is theoretically ruled out given the absence of the analysand, and though the egregious defects of "bad psychoanalysis" has been indexed by Albert Schweitzer (as noted above), a number of recent studies, albeit from a Freudian perspective, have suggested that psychoanalytic observations in the hands of seasoned analysts can provide persuasively meaningful and compelling insight into the psychodynamic factors at work in author and text,[94] e.g., the work of David Halperin on Ezekiel, fulfilling as it were an observation of Bernhard Anderson in his classic *Understanding the Old Testament*, that "Ezekiel *himself* was an unusual person whose psychic peculiarities make a fascinating psychological study."[95]

4. Biblical religious phenomena constitute a fourth area of inquiry in which a Jungian psycho-hermeneutical inquiry can enhance biblical understanding. Though Jung himself did not explore the range of religious phenomena to be found in the Bible in detail, he did manage to make passing reference to many of them, providing an occasional suggestion on their importance from a psychological perspective, and in effect outlining an agenda for future work. In his essay on "Freud and Jung: Contrasts," in which he justifies his interest in religion and its various manifestations, Jung offers the hint of a psychological interpretation of rites of initiation without mentioning baptism in particular, yet clearly

alluding to the biblical phenomenon of baptism in the spirit: "For thousands of years rites of initiation have been teaching rebirth from the spirit; yet, strangely enough, man forgets again and again the meaning of divine procreation."[96] Here as at numerous points through the Jungian corpus, he points the way to a psychological hermeneutic of ritual practice (such as footwashing, eucharist, burnt offering, purification rites), of mystical experience (e.g., visions, dreams, prophecy, photisms, auditions, inspiration, revelation, the inner light, and *enthousiasmos*), of religious states ("twice-born religion," *metanoia, kenosis,* martyrdom, and the experience of sin, guilt, forgiveness, grace, and sanctification), religious practices (prayer, glossolalia) and religious experiences (miracles, transfiguration, resurrection).

5. The pathogenic and therapeutic elements and effects in the Bible are a fifth dimension of the text of special interest to Jung that can be illumined by a psychological hermeneutic. John Dourley in his book, *The Illness That We Are: A Jungian Critique of Christianity,* identifies specific pathogenic deficiencies in Christianity that, for our purposes, are equally characteristic of the Bible or of its traditional interpretation. In *Answer to Job* Jung identifies and addresses some of these elements, but it is the task of a psychologically oriented hermeneutic to amplify the work already done by feminist and ideological critics in identifying the dark biases that enjoy advocacy in certain biblical texts. Dourley provides a starting point for such an undertaking with the pathogenic elements he identifies: (1) the "sacrosanct unintelligibility of religious language"; (2) the "systematic blindness to God within"; (3) the systematic exclusion of four realities from the God-concept: matter, the feminine, the "dark side," and the sexual-instinctual; and (4) the creation of a "militant monotheistic faith that kills."

The therapeutic dimension of the text is not one ordinarily explicated by biblical hermeneutics, but is indigenous to a Jungian understanding of the text and would constitute a special telos of a psycho-hermeneutical approach. For Jung the goal of religion in all of its manifestations, including Scripture, is the *cura animarum,* the care and cure of souls. In his essay on "The State of Psychotherapy Today" Jung writes that "religions are psychotherapeutic systems in the truest sense of the word. . . . They express the whole range of the psychic problem in mighty images;

they are the avowal and recognition of the soul, and at the same time the revelation of the soul's nature,"[97] and as we have noted earlier, they provide models of individuation. In approaching the therapeutic elements and potentiable effects of the Bible, a psychological hermeneutic can learn from the work of pastoral counselors Donald Capps, *Biblical Approaches to Pastoral Counseling*, Wayne Oates, *The Bible in Pastoral Care*, and Carroll A. Wise, *Psychiatry and the Bible*.

6. Biblical ethics is a sixth area of inquiry to which a psychological hermeneutic can contribute. Though a definitive work has yet to be written on the "ethics of consciousness" advocated by Jung, it is clear that he finds analogues for such an ethic in the life of Paul, as he indicates in his introduction to Erich Neumann's *Depth Psychology and a New Ethic*, as well as in a variant logion of Jesus from the fifth-century Codex Bezae at Luke 6:4: "Man, if indeed thou knowest what thou doest, thou art blessed; but if thou knowest not, thou art cursed, and a transgressor of the law." Jung comments, "here the moral criterion is *consciousness*, and not law or convention."[98] The spectrum of ethical postures in the Bible, from the deontological ethics of the law codes, to the love-ethic of the Johannine Christ, to the ethics of the spirit in Paul would benefit from a psychological approach that sought to understand the habits and predilections of the psyche as well as the archetypal urgings that are coming to expression in the various ethical modalities and symbol systems in the Bible.

7. The biblical reader and interpreter would also fall within the spectrum of inquiry for a psycho-hermeneutical approach to the text. Although Jung does not take up the concerns of current Reader-Response criticism, which focuses on the contribution of the reader to the construction (even the creation) of the text, Jung does acknowledge the fact of readers shaping texts. In his more cynical moments, he admits that "as we know, anything can be authorized out of the Bible,"[99] but more constructively he develops the theory of psychological types to account for the diverse renderings a common set of data enjoys from different interpreters, a fact also explored by Cedric Johnson in *The Psychology of Biblical Interpretation*. The special task of a psychological hermeneutic would be to examine the conscious and unconscious objectives and motives at work in the psyche of the reader, commenting on

both the effect of the text on the reader and the reciprocal meta-
morphosing effect of the reader on the text.

8. Biblical Psychology as defined in the eighteenth- and nineteenth-century works, such as Franz Delitzsch's *A System of
Biblical Psychology* (1861), is the discipline devoted to articulating
the biblical view(s) of the origin, nature, and destiny of the psy-
che/soul. A contemporary psychological hermeneutic would certainly include this objective in its agenda, not only as a matter of
record, but as a possible source of insight for contemporary
self-understanding. Jung spends no time at all reconstructing the
biblical model of the psyche, since he is so caught up in the
Herculean task of constructing his own. It is clear, however, that
his own model bears what appears to be a telling resemblance to
that of the Bible. Jung appears in many respects to be a "biblical
mensch," as evidenced in the "biblical" character of his *Weltbild*,
with its concern for the soul, its sense of destiny or call, its openness to the wisdom of dreams, revelations, and visions, its appreciation of the interplay between good and evil, its appreciation of
the sequence of sin and grace in human experience, and its sense
of the numinous. A psycho-hermeneutic might take notice of this
comparison, first identifying and clarifying the biblical model of
the psyche, second, inquiring into the extent that this model
might still be operative in Jung's thought in specific, and in
Western culture in general, and third, raising the question
whether the biblical model of the psyche provides a translatable
corrective or paradigm for modern and post-modern models.

C. *Method for a Jungian Psycho-Hermeneutical Approach to the
Bible.* In his book, *The Bible and the Psyche*, Jungian analyst
Edward Edinger writes, "The events of the Bible, although presented as history, psychologically understood are archetypal
images, that is, pleromatic events that repeatedly erupt into spa-
tio-temporal manifestation and require an individual ego to live
them out. As we read these stories with an openness to their
unconscious reverberations we recognize them to be relevant to
our own most private experience."[100] This statement summarizes
Jung's primary hermeneutical goal, to bring the "metaphysical"
"within the range of experience"[101] and to "take the "thought-
forms that have become historically fixed" and "try to melt them

down again and pour them into moulds of immediate experience."[102] Though a psycho-hermeneutical approach to the Bible from a Jungian perspective will utilize the findings of historical-literary critical research and focus on the specific hermeneutical tasks enumerated in the preceding section, its ultimate goal is to relate the text to the life experience of the reader and the reading community, diverting the reader from the tendency, for example, to talk of "Christ's cross" "out there," rather than "discover our own cross."[103] "In religious matters," Jung writes, "it is a well-known fact the we cannot understand a thing until we have experienced it inwardly."[104]

The two methods Jung developed for this "final" hermeneutical step of relating the text to lived experience are the processes of "amplification" and "active imagination." Though originally designed for the interpretation of dream material in the clinical context, they are equally applicable in the "investigation of psychologems, mythologems, and psychic structures of all kinds,"[105] rooted in the assumption that "the eternal truths cannot be transmitted 'mechanically' in every epoch they must be born anew from the human psyche."[106]

The hermeneutical method of amplification aims at eliciting the associations the text has evoked within the reader. It proceeds at both the subjective (personal) and objective (collective) level, searching both for the personal meaning the text may have catalyzed in the reader as well as the larger transpersonal "collective" meanings it may have inspired. Although at the personal level a psycho-hermeneutical approach can do little more than alert the individual reader to the potentiable personal meanings in the text, it can at the collective level be of assistance in three ways. First, it can locate the collective imagery of the Bible within the powerful glossary of archetypal images that recur in the art, literature, and religions of the world, where they can be seen to provide guidance and direction for individuals and whole cultures, as they do in the Bible. Second, it can seek on the basis of its research in comparative mythology and folklore to proffer an interpretation of biblical imagery, resting on Jung's psychological observation that the interpretation of art cannot rest on the artist, but remains a task for the future: "Being essentially the instrument of his work, [the artist] is subordinate to it, and we have no right to expect him to interpret it for us. He has done his utmost by giving it form and must leave the interpretation to others and to the future."[107] Third, a psychological hermeneutic can seek to draw out untapped meanings, resident in the text, that remain to be identified and articulated, especially in "openly symbolic" texts, such as Goethe's *Faust II*, where meaning can exceed the conscious intent and awareness of the author.[108] Thus, the responsibility of the interpreter, humanly and professionally, is to occasion the birth of those meanings not yet consciously noted and articulated, for the good of the author, the good of the reader, and the good of the broader humanity for whom, according to Jung, the image has emerged and "been revealed" from the depths of the objective unconscious in the first place.

The hermeneutical method of active imagination takes the interpretive process one step further through a process of "translating" the amplified message into new forms. The forms can range from painting, dancing, storytelling, and clay,[109] to stained-glass windows, liturgy, musical cantatas, mystery plays, and religious pageants, or even new translations or versions of the text. Its purpose is, in Jung's classical formulation, to enable the reader to "dream the myth onwards and give it a modern dress."[110]

The presupposition of the method is that because "a living symbol expresses something that is not fully conscious, or able yet to become fully conscious"[111] the imagination, catalyzed by a text, is enlisted to search for the unconscious content the symbol may have evoked in the self. To do this, conscious thinking is not enough. What is required is a method involving fantasy (regarded by Peter Homans as the primary psychological activity in Jung's psychological hermeneutic)[112] and reduced ego functioning so that the wisdom of the unconscious, can come into play. As Jung observes, "often the hands know how to solve a riddle with which the intellect has wrestled in vain."[113] From a psychological standpoint, something is "gained in translation" rather than lost, since each of the techniques employed represents a curiously discrete angle of vision which can perceive and draw things out of the text other faculties and modes of expression would never catch. The potter, the dancer, the storyteller, the musician, playwright, and preacher all come to the text with *sui generis* aptitudes and appetites that render specific dimensions of the text susceptible to their visions and interpretations. As a result of this active imaginal dialectic with the text, which Janet Dallett likens to the unremitting dialogue of Tevya with God in *Fiddler on the Roof*,[114] new dimensions of the text are unconcealed and new depths of the text are realized in concrete form, and in many instances, as in the case of religious art, literature, liturgy, music, or drama, it becomes the *primary* mediator of the meaning of the text, even more than the text itself, the "modern dress" in which the *mythos* is clothed.

The goal of a psycho-hermeneutical approach will be to integrate these methods with the panoply of critical methods extant in the field, but at the same time seek to bend the hermeneutical effort as a whole into the service of the ultimate goal it serves from a Jungian perspective, namely to "create more and more consciousness. As far as we can discern," Jung writes, "the sole purpose of human existence is to kindle a light in the darkness of mere being."[115]

❧ 1 ❧

Jacob—A Study in Individuation

D. ANDREW KILLE

In this essay, we will examine the cycle of stories about Jacob [Gen. 25:19–35:29] in the light of C. G. Jung's theory of individuation. We will set aside questions about origins, history, and development of the text in order to look at the elements of the narrative as we have it. Jacob's story is one example of the mythical motif of the hero's journey, which has at its core the archetypal movement of individuation.

Jung's *archetypes* are the "primordial images common to humanity"[1]—structures of the psyche which shape individual experience. They are only *patterns* of experience, without specific content, until the specific experience of the individual brings them forth.[2] Although they are the source of myth and symbolism, they are not identified with specific mythological images or motifs; they are solely "the tendency to form such representations of a motif—representations that can vary a great deal in detail without losing their basic pattern."[3]

The archetypes, being unconscious, are unknowable in themselves. They can only be seen in dream images, fantasies, or when they are *projected* out of the unconscious in such a way that the conscious mind can experience them. Projection is "an unconscious, automatic process whereby a content that is unconscious to the subject transfers itself to an object, so that it seems to belong to that object."[4] One arena for such projection is in myths and stories—"in fact the whole of mythology could be taken as a sort of projection of the collective unconscious."[5]

Even when a story shows no concern for "psychological" issues (as biblical stories do not), the collective patterning and projecting processes are still operating. In fact, as Jung remarked about modern literature, "in general, it is the non- psychological novel [in contrast to the 'psychological novel'] that offers the richest opportunities . . . such a tale is constructed against a background of unspoken psychological assumptions, and the more unconscious the author is of them, the more this background reveals itself. . . ."[6] Jung also cautions against psychologizing, noting that the critic who uses psychological notions to bring out aspects of the complexity of human experience may provide insights, but that the critic who imposes his psychological scheme on the literary text will in all likelihood limit and distort.[7]

Jung identified several archetypes, three of which are most pertinent to our investigation here: the *shadow*, the *anima*, and the *Self*.

Rejected and undervalued aspects of the individual psyche are repressed into the personal unconscious where they reside as the *shadow*. The shadow is made up of "little-known attributes and qualities of the ego," not only the negative, but the unrealized positive.[8] The shadow is most often projected onto others; we are all familiar with the person who sees negative qualities in everyone except him/her self.[9]

The *anima* expresses itself as a feminine personality in a man, and is easily projected onto a woman.[10] In her positive aspect, the anima serves as the mediator between the ego and the unconscious.[11] She is the archetype of "life itself."[12] This is Jung's reason for naming her the anima, from the Latin for soul. This soul is not the theological "soul," but the principle of life, that which animates.[13]

The final and comprehensive archetype is the *Self*. Present from the very beginning as the unconscious possibility, it is both the guiding principle and the final goal of the total personality. It is "the completest expression of that fateful combination we call individuality," encompassing both conscious and unconscious elements.[14] As guide, the Self is the source of the inner drive to psychic growth, the sender of dreams, and a regulating center.[15] The Self is expressed in images and symbols of totality, especially religious ones: the Christ, the Buddha, and the Son of Man share this dimension of the "total human being."[16] The encounter with the Self is experienced as a meeting with the divine.

It is essential for psychological growth and maturity that an individual recognize and relate to these three archetypes; this process of encounter Jung called *individuation*. Individuation is "the process by which a person becomes a psychological 'individual,' that is, a separate, indivisible unity or 'whole.'"[17] It is "the conscious realization and integration of all the possibilities immanent in the individual."[18]

Individuation does not follow a linear path, but it does involve certain characteristic developments.[19] The first stage is involved with the development of consciousness and the ego. As a necessity of the connectedness of ego and shadow, the shadow, also, is developed, but remains unconscious.

The next stage involves turning toward the unconscious, encountering and relating to the archetypes there. This work begins with the shadow, the most personal part of the unconscious. In dealing with archetypes, there are two reciprocal dangers: one, that the ego will continue to repress the unconscious, the other, that the ego will identify with the unconscious, becoming absorbed and ruled by the archetypes.[20] Along with this, there is the danger that arises out of the dual nature of the archetypes. "Every personification of the unconscious . . . has both a light and a dark aspect."[21] The shadow has both positive and negative elements.

The way then leads to encounters with the anima, which, as we observed above, is the guide to the inner world. The final encounter, as well as the goal, of individuation is with the Self, which has been present unconsciously from the beginning and only now can be realized in relationship to consciousness. "[O]ne can regard the individuation process as a growing of the ego out of the Self and as a re-rooting in it."[22]

THE JACOB CYCLE

The literary-historical composition of the Jacob narrative cycle does not concern us here. It has long been recognized that it contains elements from many traditions, gathered in the J, E, and P strands of the Pentateuchal tradition.[23] Embedded in the narratives are various aetiological explanations for the names of people (e.g., Esau [Edom], Jacob [Israel] and his sons), places (e.g., Beth-el; Mizpah; Jabbok; Mahanaim), and of a food taboo (eating the sinew on the thigh).

It is the narrative form of Jacob's story that concerns us. It is, of course, one link in the story of the patriarchs, extending from Abraham through Joseph, comprising the major part of the book of Genesis. The story of Jacob is shaped by the overall concern of the book and the Pentateuch as a whole—as David Clines has suggested, "*the partial fulfillment—which implies also the partial non-fulfillment—of the promise to or blessing of the patriarchs.*"[24] The three dimensions of this blessing—children, land, and the relationship with God—figure prominently in Jacob's story.

Michael Fishbane notes how the theme of blessing (*barakh* and its cognate noun *birakah*—blessing) links together the segments of the Jacob story. His analysis of the structure of the cycle can be seen in the diagram on the following page.[25]

The story of Jacob is framed by genealogical lists (*toledot*) of the excluded sons, Ishmael and Esau, and links Jacob in the succession of the patriarchs. Similar structural links can be seen in episodes of the narrative, the encounter at the Jabbok and the meeting with Esau.[26]

Using the framework outlined above (omitting the interludes at B and B'),[27] let us note how Jacob's story, full of blessing and struggle, can be read as a story of one man's path to transformation and individuation.

A: BIRTH OF A HERO: THE TWINS (25:19–34).

Jacob's story begins with a theme familiar to biblical birth narratives, the barrenness (*'aqarah*) of his mother. Seen elsewhere in the birth stories of Isaac and Joseph (Gen. 18:1–15; 29:31; 30:23–24), it carries here, as in Isaac's case, a threat to the continuation of God's promise of descendants. The motif of the barren mother is often associated in myth with the birth of a hero.[28]

Myths of the hero themselves are varied expressions of the archetypal journey of individuation. The difficulties encountered in the birth and childhood of the hero express how hard it is to come into consciousness.[29]

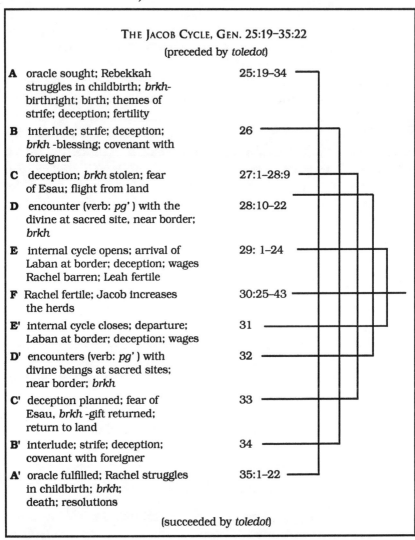

THE JACOB CYCLE, GEN. 25:19–35:22

(preceded by *toledot*)

A oracle sought; Rebekkah struggles in childbirth; *brkh*-birthright; birth; themes of strife; deception; fertility — 25:19–34

B interlude; strife; deception; *brkh* -blessing; covenant with foreigner — 26

C deception; *brkh* stolen; fear of Esau; flight from land — 27:1–28:9

D encounter (verb: *pgʼ*) with the divine at sacred site, near border; *brkh* — 28:10–22

E internal cycle opens; arrival of Laban at border; deception; wages Rachel barren; Leah fertile — 29: 1–24

F Rachel fertile; Jacob increases the herds — 30:25–43

E' internal cycle closes; departure; Laban at border; deception; wages — 31

D' encounters (verb: *pgʼ*) with divine beings at sacred sites; near border; *brkh* — 32

C' deception planned; fear of Esau, *brkh* -gift returned; return to land — 33

B' interlude; strife; deception; covenant with foreigner — 34

A' oracle fulfilled; Rachel struggles in childbirth; *brkh*; death; resolutions — 35:1–22

(succeeded by *toledot*)

When Rebekah does give birth, it is to twins, who are as different as can be: Esau, the hairy, and Jacob, "at the heel" (*baʻaqēv*). Twins appear as a mythological symbol for psychic complementarity, the image of self division.[30] In the myths of the Winnebago Indians, the Twins together comprise one person; united in the womb, they are separated at birth, and prove difficult to reunite. One, named "Flesh," is "acquiescent, mild, and without initiative, the other, "Stump," is dynamic and rebellious.[31] It is not difficult to see parallels in Esau and Jacob, who are likewise described in complementary terms. Jacob and Esau personify the dual nature of the psyche, divided between ego and shadow. Esau is related to the instinctual, animal world, not only in his appearance, but in his occupation. He is the "firstborn," wholly included in the unconscious, acting out of instinct.[32] Out of hunger, he is willing to forfeit his birthright (*bekorah*—note the inversion of *birakah*; cognates include *bekor* [m.] and *bekirah* [f.]—firstborn).

Jacob, on the other hand, struggles with his brother, first in the womb, then for the birthright. His is the ego struggling into consciousness, which has to fight for its position against the pull of the collective.[33] In his theft of the birthright, he takes control of the psyche, but at the loss of the unity of the Twins.[34] There will be a price to pay, for though the ego and the shadow are separate, they are "inextricably bound up together."[35]

C: THE STOLEN BLESSING (27:1–28:9).

Having stolen the birthright, Jacob compounds his disdain for his brother by conspiring to take his blessing (*birakah*). He is aided in this by his mother Rebekah, who, acting with the knowledge of the prophecy given to her by God (25:23), dares to seek its fulfillment in totally unexpected ways. As his mother, the first bearer of the projection of Jacob's anima,[36] Rebekah serves to urge him toward the realization of his inborn identity promised in the oracle of his birth, the potential of the Self. She expresses the simultaneous "wisdom and folly" of the anima in urging the psyche toward life in sometimes chaotic ways.[37]

In his deception of Isaac, Jacob separates even farther from identification with his unconscious origins. Such is his sense of disconnection with his father that his only objection to deceiving Isaac arises out of a concern for his own safety (v.12). Yet there is a kind of fundamental honesty; he does not deny that he is tricking his father. This kind of psychological honesty will be a prerequisite for growth.[38] He knowingly deceives his father, and receives the blessing without truly understanding what it means.[39]

The ego's further devaluing of the instinctual, even to achieve a worthy goal, brings about a deeper split in the personality. The more the shadow is repressed, the more it will fight back; Esau hates his brother and "comforts himself" with planning to kill

Jacob.[40] For his own safety, Jacob must leave his beloved mother and home and flee into the unknown.

D: ENCOUNTER WITH THE DIVINE AT BETH-EL (28:10–22).

Jacob flees into the wilderness. This is the first movement in the process of individuation, separation from original identification with the unconscious. It is a necessary step, but separation is "finally no solution."[41] The wilderness is an archetypal symbol of the step into the unknown, the beginning of the journey of individuation.[42] It is in the wilderness that Jacob, the quiet tent-dweller, finds his comfortable world shattered. He has lost his home, his family, and even, as one Rabbinic tradition remarks, his clothing and possessions.[43] In this time of suffering, Jacob begins, for the first time in the cycle, a direct relationship with God, "entering a new phase of his heroic identity."[44]

At the beginning of the hero's journey, the hero often meets a "protective figure" who provides a promise of protection against the dangers.[45] Jacob's protector is none other than God; the meeting is at Beth-el, the "House of God."

"The place" marks (as Peniel will again, in chapter 32) a boundary which is not only geographic, but personal. Even as Jacob crosses outwardly out of Canaan, he crosses inwardly into his unconscious. At the boundaries, in need both inwardly and outwardly, Jacob encounters the divine and emerges as a more whole person.[46] It is here at the border, in the wilderness, that Jacob has his dream of the "ladder" (*sullam*). The term, found only here in the Bible, is perhaps better translated "ramp,"[47] and very likely uses the image of the ziggurat to give content to the archetypal symbol of the "ascent."[48]

The ascent to heaven is characteristic of mystical visions and ecstatic states. Whatever context or values may accompany the ascents, they "always signify a transcending of the human and a penetration into higher cosmic levels."[49] Shamanic initiations contain variations on the theme: climbing ropes, trees, mountains, a spiral ladder, or the rainbow.[50] Indeed, ziggurats sometimes were painted in rainbow colors, and had names that linked heaven and earth.[51] The Rabbis tried in various ways to connect the vision to the ultimate place of "ascent"—Jerusalem—by envisioning the "ramp" as arching from Beersheba to Beth-el, curving over the Temple.[52]

Jacob's dream is highly significant. As Elie Wiesel points out, he is "the first dreamer in biblical history. Abraham had visions; Jacob had dreams."[53] Dreams are a primary way that the conscious mind comes to know the unconscious archetypes. Jacob's dream symbol of the ascent to heaven, coming to him when he is a fugitive in the wilderness, at a low point of alienation, is a "classic image of the Ego-Self axis . . . a vision of its [the ego's] connection to the Self."[54] Jacob begins to be aware for the first time of a connection to something beyond his own ego; he gains a vision of the possibility of a new consciousness, a new center of personality.[55]

The dream is *numinous*, that is, it has great energy, fascination, and a "spiritual" quality—a characteristic of archetypal symbols, especially of the Self.[56] Jacob awakes with a feeling of fear and awe, and the conviction that "the LORD is in this place" (v. 16–17).

The consciousness prefigured by the dream is only beginning to come into being. Jacob has a long way to go before he achieves it. He can only observe the "ramp"; he is not yet ready for the ascent.[57] As he awakes, he acknowledges a new connection with God, but it is a conditional one. He vows to set up a shrine and give a tithe of his gains, if God will provide him with safety, food, clothing, and a return home (v. 20).[58]

E, F, E': In Haran: Love and Work (29–31).

After crossing the boundary into the unknown, Jacob makes his way to Haran. In myth, after moving out of the familiar, the hero faces a series of trials, which can take almost any form.[59] These trials correspond to the tasks of individuation, of recognizing and integrating the shadow and the anima. The biblical text does not describe Jacob's inward life, but we can discern in the outward events some evidence of his inner growth.

Meeting his kinsfolk at a well, Jacob immediately falls in love with Rachel. "Love at first sight" happens when the anima is projected outwardly onto a woman. If it remains projected, if the man does not recognize his inner anima, he will remain incapable of authentic relationship. If, however, he can acknowledge and honor this part of his psyche, the anima becomes a mediator between the ego and the Self.[60]

Jacob's willingness to work seven years for Rachel is an indication that he is moving beyond projection—"being in love with being in love"—into an authentic relationship with her.[61] Yet it is precisely at this point that his shadow ambushes him. "As long as the conflict is not resolved (flight means repression) it will be constellated in life by a repetition."[62] Jacob's trickery in dealing with Esau and Isaac is now echoed in Laban's substitution of Leah for Rachel. Martin Buber comments, "In his place of exile, in which God certainly shields him but does not withhold from him mishaps, Jacob gets to see with his own eyes what guile perpetuated against a man by his own kin really is." Jacob's question, "why have you deceived me?" is answered "we do not give the younger before the firstborn (bekirah)."[63] The deceiver is deceived, and Jacob has the opportunity to meet his shadow face to face.

His love for Rachel is such that he is willing to work seven more years for her. Jacob's growing capacity for genuine related-ness is also shown by his favoring Rachel even when she is not able to fulfill the expected role of bearing children. When at last she does bear a son (again we find the theme of barrenness ('aqerah) in the birth of a hero), that son is Joseph and he will be the next bearer of the birakah. It is out of the relationship of growing consciousness that the promise will be carried on.

In the meantime, Jacob devotes himself to the task of establishing himself firmly in the world. He gains wives, chil-dren, and herds, and has served Laban long and well. His strengthened ego, though still separated from deeper uncon-scious drives and instincts, can now draw upon the shadow side, turning the deceitful trickster into a successful entrepre-neur.[64] He is doing quite well, and could easily have exchanged the promise at Beth-el for a long and prosperous life of ease.

But something begins to stir in Jacob that will not let him rest. In the "second half" of his life, the need to integrate the lost parts of his psyche begins to emerge. His outer work has been a success; now he must deal with the inner. In part, Jacob's deci-sion to return to his home arises from outward factors—Laban's sons are growing jealous of his wealth—but it is above all the command of the divine, coming again in a dream, that sets him on the homeward journey. He is learning the meaning of the birakah. The relationship with God is not merely a promise of wealth and posterity; it means that when God says, "Go!" he must obey. He can go no further in reconciling with his unconscious without a reconciliation with Esau; for the sake of his soul he must make restitution for his deceit.[65]

On the way, he is pursued by Laban and his kinsfolk. Laban has also had a message from God, and offers to make a covenant. The reconciliation with Laban is another step in reintegrating Jacob's psyche. He had related to Laban, who stood in Isaac's place, as a son to his Father. Now Jacob is no longer identified with or subservient to the Father; nor is he completely cut off from relationship. He and Laban can meet each other as equals, and let each other go in peace.[66] Jacob is beginning to assimilate the scattered fragments of his life.

D': ENCOUNTERS WITH THE DIVINE AT MAHANAIM AND PENIEL (32).

Again at the boundary between sacred and profane space, Jacob encounters the divine. At Mahanaim (*two camps*) he sees a group of angels. The Rabbis saw the "two camps" as being Jacob's and the angels,'[67] demonstrating how "biblical history . . . unfolds on two planes"—the personal and the divine.[68] The outer world and the inner world are parallel; "personal development and the experience of God are . . . not to be separated from each other."[69]

It is a changed Jacob who prepares with fear and trembling to meet with his estranged brother. He acknowledges his dependence on God in a prayer far different from his bargaining at Bethel; he prepares to accept whatever may come. His lavish gifts for Esau are evidence of his maturity. Where as a youth struggling for domination he took what was rightfully Esau's, he is now willing to sacrifice his ego power for the sake of reconciliation.[70]

It is no accident of editing that Jacob's preparations are interrupted by the encounter at the Jabbok; "the experience of self, god, life, and faith are interwoven."[71] Left alone by the river in the darkness, Jacob faces his greatest test.

A river can be a symbol of a boundary with the unconscious,[72] and it is here, in the dark (also a symbol of the unconscious)[73] that a desperate struggle takes place. *Someone* ('ish is indefinite here)[74] appears, and wrestles with Jacob.

Who is this nocturnal antagonist? Speculations have been endless: "'ish in the text, Midrash and commentators make him an angel, Jacob himself calls him *God*, a name accepted by the 'man.'"[75] Is he Michael or Sariel,[76] Esau's guardian angel,[77] or a prophetic vision or dream?[78] Is he a corporeal being,[79] a dream image,[80] or even, as later Christian commentators suggested, Jesus himself?[81] Many commentators suggest a parallel to protective river spirits,[82] but Hendel states he is "neither a night-demon or a river God; Jacob names him in v. 31 as elohim."[83]

The parallel in Hos. 12:4–5 is no more clear:

> In the womb he supplanted his brother,
> and as a man he contended with God,
> he contended with an angel and prevailed.

Who, then, is this someone? Perhaps all of these and more. For this battle at the Jabbok tells of an encounter with the deepest places of Jacob's soul, peopled with the archetypal forces of the shadow and the Self. Jacob is, as Wiesel says, "attacked by his own guardian angel. The mysterious aggressor? The other half of Jacob's split self. The side of him that harbored doubts about his mission, his future, his *raison d'être*. . . ."[84] Jacob must struggle on one hand with the shadow side of his personality, all that he has repressed, avoided, and fled from. In order to embrace the totality of his life, he must come to grips with his deceit, his injuring his father and brother, his theft of the birthright, with "the 'Esau' he carries within him."[85]

On the other hand, this encounter is more than a human crisis of conscience. It is more than Jacob's encounter with his personal shadow. "Complete internalization of the struggle does not reflect the biblical intent. The text tells of God's role in Jacob's renewal; Jacob becomes Israel only with God's help."[86]

Jacob's assailant is none other than the divine, the totality of the Self. The variety of interpretations offered for the identity of the someone is expressive of the multiplicity of symbolic representations of the archetype of the Self.[87] In this light, the Christian association of the "one" with Christ is not so far-fetched, since Christ is also an image of the Self.[88]

The self, like all archetypes, has both a positive and a negative dimension. Positively, it includes all the aspects of the psyche into the totality of the personality. In its destructive form, the Self is a devourer of the ego. The ego, which previously has denied the unconscious (repression), now must, in meeting the totality of the unconscious, struggle against being absorbed by it (identification). If the ego can meet the Self so that "it will not prevail," and yet not "let it go" back into unconscious repression (32:26–27), a transformation takes place: "the onslaught of instinct then becomes an experience of divinity, provided that man does not succumb to it and follow it blindly, but defends his humanity against the animal nature of the divine power."[89]

The power of the Adversary is shown in his wounding of Jacob. The purpose is not to destroy, however, but to test. Jacob's wound is that of anyone who touches spiritual reality so deeply.[90] It is a mark of the lessening of egocentric power, sacrificed to the deeper center of the Self.[91]

The depth of Jacob's transformation is confirmed in his renaming. "When one knows what the name meant then in Israel, one will recognize . . . not only a renaming, but an intervention (*Eingriff*), a transformation."[92] Throughout the story the words *blessing* (*brk*) and *name* (*shem*) are interwoven. One's name signifies one's identity. "Jacob" is the ego-name; "Israel," the Self-name. In order to be blessed, "Jacob" must give way; out of this ego-sacrifice "Israel" is born. Jacob's offer of his name, *ya'aqov*, a confession and acceptance of his former identity as "he-who-lies-in-ambush-at-the-heel," is necessary for the blessing.[93] Jacob cannot enter the full realization of his identity by repressing his past; it must be included and transformed.[94]

The Adversary must remain nameless. As the Self, the totality of consciousness, it is unnameable.[95] One Rabbinic tradition held that angels did not have permanent names; their names changed according to the tasks they were to perform.[96] This would correspond to the fact that the archetype of the Self can never be contained in any one manifestation; it will be constellated anew in each life-situation. A tantalizing suggestion in *Pirke Rab Eliezar* is that this angel's name is Israel, the same as Jacob's new name.[97] As this new name identifies the new personality centered in the Self, rather than the ego, it would be a more than fitting name for the agent of the Self who bestows it.

With the name comes the right to the blessing. Jacob/Israel can now be the full recipient of the *birakah*. What he had taken by deceit and trickery was not his; the full blessing is won by his openness and struggle.[98] His courage in facing the psychological struggle has made him a worthy bearer of the promise. "A genuine relationship with God does not reside in mere passivity, rejoicing in election and waiting on providence . . . ; it entails as well personal effort, a striving, wrestling with the divine will and purposes."[99]

C': Reunion with Esau (33).

The reconciliation which had been forged inwardly during the night now takes effect outwardly as Jacob/Israel prepares to meet Esau.[100] Esau himself seems to have undergone some transformation in the intervening years. Gone is the murderous rage; he embraces Jacob and weeps. Jacob/Israel sees in the face of his brother the image of the wrestling reconciler, and after all these years of separation, he offers Esau a gift or "blessing" (*birkhah*, v. 11), to atone for his theft of the blessing (*birakah*). The circle is complete; the twins are again one. It should be noted that this reconciliation is not complete; there appears to be some residual mistrust between the brothers. Individuation is never complete, either. "Individuation is a process, not a realized goal."[101]

A': Return to Beth-el (35:1–22).

The remaining episodes of the Jacob cycle tell us little more about Jacob/Israel's journey of individuation. Jacob/Israel travels through the land of his birth, settling at Shechem for a time before returning at last to Beth-el, the place of his dream long ago. At that place where he first became conscious of his connection to the Self, he receives a reaffirmation of God's promise—the blessing of children, land, and the relationship with God. Strangely, even though God says "no longer shall you be called Jacob" (35:10), in the following verses he is called both Jacob (vv. 14–15, 20, 22b) and Israel (21–22a). As Wiesel puts it:

> We are explicitly forbidden to call Abraham by his former name Avram, but such is not the case for Jacob. . . . Israel would not have been Israel had he not first been Jacob, had he not carried inside himself Jacob's strange and exalted dream.[102]

From this point on, Israel is a transformed Jacob, bearing his past in a new way.

CONCLUSIONS

Jung's theory of individuation provides one rich resource for understanding Jacob's story and some dimensions of the meaning of *berakah.* We have seen how the narrative structure of the story corresponds to the stages in the cycle of individuation. The two key points in the narrative which describe an encounter with the divine at geographic boundaries coincide with encounters with the Self at the boundaries of the unconscious. Jacob's name change is a clear signal in Hebrew understanding of a change of identity, and it happens precisely at that stage in the individuation cycle where the ego ceases to be the center of personality, yielding to the transcendent center of the Self.

The recurrent theme of *birakah* is linked to the development of Jacob's consciousness, as the potential but unrealized possibility of the Self partially expressed, at first, in Jacob's one-sided ego development, and only later truly granted and made complete through struggle and ego-sacrifice.

While we do not have reports of Jacob's dealings with his shadow and anima in the text, we do have descriptions of his relationships with Laban and Rachel which hint at opportunities for such integration.

Clearly, the Jacob story is one expression of a character's journey toward wholeness. We must not forget that it is not only a story of individuation; among other things, it is also about cult shrines, place names, national origins and identity, and relations with God, clans, and other peoples.

There is a tension between archetypal symbols and their particular expression. Their expression is always conditioned by particular situations and personalities. Collective experiences are not only collective, "they hang together with the concrete situation just of this man, *his* childhood development, *his* bodily, spiritual, and soul development, *his* environment."[103] In considering archetypal dimensions, we must avoid the temptation to discard the particularities of the story to fit our "universal pattern."[104]

At the same time, we can recognize in the particular the expression of universal human experience. The power of archetypal images is that they cannot be exhausted. Each human life unfolds in the tension between that which is particular to the individual and that which is common to all.

Thus, while Jacob's story is particular in detail to the man Jacob (be he historical, mythical, or literary), it is also one expression of a "universal experience and . . . not a private mystery. While Jacob's way as a prototype is a universal way, the experience of it is private and unique for every individual."[105]

In the story of Jacob, as indeed in all stories that have power to move us, inner archetypes are projected onto symbols and figures which we can observe and to which we can relate. These symbols can become a way for us to encounter our own unconscious worlds. Jacob's story is, in a very real sense, our story; Jacob's wrestling can become our wrestling; Jacob's journey to blessing, a prompting for our own.[106]

✻2✻

Joseph's Dreams

TREVOR WATT

INTRODUCTION

With Joseph, a new mood is introduced into the Hebrew Bible. After the early myths of Genesis chapters 1–11, and then after the stories of the patriarchy, Joseph is introduced. The change has been expressed in several ways.

Elie Wiesel says: "Abraham is respected and admired; Isaac is pitied; Jacob is followed; but only Joseph is loved."[1]

Nahum Sarna describes the change in Genesis this way: "The miraculous and supernatural element is conspicuously absent . . . there are no divine revelations, no altars, no cult associations. God never intervenes openly and directly in Joseph's life as He does with Abraham, Isaac and Jacob."[2]

Dorothy Zeligs completes her study of Joseph with the comment that "Joseph is not immortalized among the twelve tribes of Israel . . . [Jacob] eliminates Joseph and puts [his sons Ephraim and Manasseh] in their father's [Joseph's] place. . . . Thus Joseph remains a son rather than the father of a tribe."[3]

Finally, Zeligs asks what the appeal of Joseph is, for he "does not have the . . . daemonic power of Abraham and Jacob . . . [or] the romantic aura of David and Solomon." She concludes that it must be "his human qualities that touch [us]."[4]

I. JOSEPH'S DREAMS

In examining the dreams of the man who represents change in the book of Genesis, I shall approach the dreams in the same way that one would the reports of a contemporary dreamer who reports a dream in verbal or written form, i.e., with all the distortions as well as with the implicit and explicit emotions.

In the first dream Joseph says to his brothers, "We were binding sheaves in the field, and lo, my sheaf arose, and stood upright; and behold, your sheaves gathered around it, and bowed down to my sheaf" (Gen. 37:7).

A. *First of all, taking the dream at face value* and looking for the metaphors, images, or themes that stand out in the manifest content, a number of possibilities occur: "one-upmanship," "domination/submission," "worship me," "King Sheaf and the subject sheaves," "the erect and the depressed," "the brat," and "rise and fall."

Following Jung's suggestion that, on the one hand, a dream depicts in image and symbol the current state of the psyche from the perspective of the unconscious, and that, on the other hand, the dream perspective is frequently compensatory to the conscious one, it is apparent that Joseph has major issues with power, sibling rivalry, masculine identity, vulnerability and fertility (the seeds of barley grain).

In a second dream, Joseph reports that "the sun the moon and eleven stars were bowing down to me" (Gen. 37:9). This time the imagery changes from daily life on the farm to celestial imagery. There is an expansion of perspective and a heightening of the intense emotions. Some themes are: "the Star (a metaphor)," "starry-eyed," "star light, star bright," "the stars in their course," "all things shall bow," "son of the universe," "the universe revolves around me," "king of the cosmos," "starry, starry night." A contemporary association is apposite: namely— "When you wish upon a star."

B. *A next step in dream reflection is to examine what is going on in the dreamer's life* at the time of the dream. In Joseph's case, no specific event is mentioned. However, if we look at Joseph's developmental stage in his life cycle, it may not be accidental that the point is made about his being seventeen years of age. This suggests that he reached puberty in the previous year and so as the second youngest brother of twelve, he is looking for masculine identity, for a role in his adult family as a middle child, and for an acceptance of himself as a middle child. Some of these issues are accentuated by his being born into what in more recent times has been termed "a tilted family," one in which all the siblings are the same sex.[5]

C. *A third step in dream reflection is to look at the dreamer in terms of the themes, strengths, and issues* of their family of origin. This is particularly important in the case of Joseph.

1. Joseph's great grandparents all came from Ur of the Chaldees (near modern day Basra). The most significant ancestor for Joseph was his great grandfather *Abraham.* Abraham was a brilliant entrepreneur, trading between Mesopotamia, Canaan (where he made a home where Joseph was born), and Egypt (where Joseph spent all but the first seventeen years of his life). His new god had spoken to him in a vivid dream about a covenant which the god would make with him to ensure that Abraham would possess the land of Canaan and that it would remain in the possession of his descendants after him forever.

2. Joseph's most significant grandparent was *Isaac.* The best known family story about him was when his father Abraham was about to fall into Canaanite religious practice by turning Isaac, his only son, into a child sacrifice (the Akeda). Isaac was saved by another divine revelation to Abraham as the knife was about to be plunged into the son.

3. Joseph's father *Jacob* was the younger of twin sons born to Isaac and Rebekah. Jacob was a mother's son. After the inevitable family conflict which ensued from this split favoritism, Jacob tricked his older brother out of his patriarchal birthright but then had to flee, to save his life, to his mother's brother in Mesopotamia.

4. During this Mesopotamian period of Jacob's life, he fell in love with his cousin *Rachel* but was tricked into first marrying her elder sister Leah before marrying his beloved Rachel, who became Joseph's mother.

Rachel is depicted as a capable, independent young woman who can hold her own with rough male shepherds at the watering hole for the flocks. She is described as beautiful, attractive, resourceful, and also as being as capable of being a trickster like her father Laban or her aunt Rebekah (who is Joseph's grandmother). Rachel was a secure, loved wife throughout her adult life.

5. Rachel got pregnant only after bartering with her rival sister for an aphrodisiac/fertility herbal root. She named her son *Joseph* which means something like "God has added another son—at last." Understandably he was doted on by his mother. At this stage, his father also seemed to favor his youngest son—having been one himself. In fact his father made for him what has been called a coat of many colors, a long sleeved robe and an ornamented tunic.[6] Whatever it was, it marked Joseph as special.

Growing up, Joseph would have slept in his mother's tent as did the sons of Leah. A special section of each tent was reserved for Jacob. It meant that Joseph grew up in a quieter atmosphere compared to the noise of his elder brothers in the other tent.

Joseph's specialness in the eyes of his mother, according to Zeligs, is characterized by Freud: "A man who has been the indisputable favorite of his mother keeps for life the feeling of a conqueror, that confidence of success that often induces real success."[7] Clearly Freud himself fell into this category.

About seven years later, Rachel again got pregnant and died giving birth to Benjamin. This must have been a shocking and devastating loss to Joseph as he was deprived of his mother's warmth and love and also of her protection from the gang of his elder brothers.

Joseph's dream occurred when Jacob was settled back in the land of Canaan as a farmer and sheep herder.

D. A fourth step in dream reflection is to look at the issues that the dreamer is currently dealing with in his or her life.

1. First of all, for ten years Joseph has been trying to cope with the devastating loss of personal power within the family. With his mother dead, the taunts, jibes, and physical abuse of his older brothers had little to restrain them on a day to day basis.

2. Joseph's sense of his own self-worth had also diminished greatly over the decade since his mother's death, as he had been placed in the tent of his mother's handmaiden. He had lost the warmth, affection, approval, and protection of his earlier years. We can safely speculate that the sons of the handmaiden would have been all too glad to have the brat and the tattle-tale knocked off his perch. In addition, they identified themselves with the aggressive elder brothers and not with the victim of aggression.

3. It is also likely that Joseph, having recently reached puberty and needing his mother's presence for this new phase of his life, re-experienced his childhood loss in an intensified form. As a result, he was in poor shape to deal with the competitive rivalry of the older, physically stronger brothers.

4. His family position as scapegoat was now established.

5. Not surprisingly, Joseph bonded with his younger, full-blooded brother, Benjamin. Benjamin was now and remained the youngest of the brothers, with all the special treatment from the father attached to him. Joseph seemed to have cared for Benjamin as a way of being true to his dead mother and as a way of giving the warmth and affection he would himself have wished to receive.

6. Joseph is described as "of beautiful form and fair to look upon." His abilities in intellect and leadership found no outlet or expression; but his air of superiority must have been unmistakable to his older brothers.

7. Joseph's pain must have arisen from the conflict between his sense of superiority and ability on the one hand and his sense of importance and awful vulnerability on the other hand.

E. *Now we are in a position to reflect* on Joseph's dreams and his family's reaction to them in Gen. 37:5–11. Here is the text:

> 5) Now Joseph had a dream, and when he told it to his brothers they only hated him the more. 6) He said to them, "Hear this dream which I have dreamed: 7) behold, we were binding sheaves in the field, and lo, my sheaf arose and stood upright; and behold, your sheaves gathered round it, and bowed down to my sheaf." 8) His brothers said to him, "Are you indeed to reign over us? Or are you indeed to have dominion over us?" So they hated him yet more for his dreams and for his words. 9) Then he dreamed another dream, and told it to his brothers, and said, "Behold, I have dreamed another dream; and behold, the sun, the moon, and eleven stars were bowing down to me." 10) But when he told it to his father and to his brothers, his father rebuked him, and said to him, "What is this dream that you have dreamed? Shall I and your mother and your brothers indeed come to bow ourselves to the ground before you?" 11) And his brothers were jealous of him, but his father kept the saying in mind.

1. First, it is noticeable that God does not figure as a partic-
ipant directly or indirectly in either dream as had occurred in
Abraham or Jacob's dreams. Second, the context, which is taken
for granted here, is that dreams were regarded as vehicles of
divine communication in the Ancient Near East. Dream interpretation was itself seen as a specialized skill, as many ancient documents testify.[8] Third, these dreams do not convey a cognitive
message in direct prose but use symbolism heavily.

2. Let us now look at the symbolism and emotion in the
dreams. In his first dream, it is clear that Joseph is trying to rec-
tify a power imbalance between himself and his brothers. Two of
the important symbolic themes are power and fertility.

The dreams can be seen as compensatory in that, whereas in
his daily life Joseph is the outsider and the scapegoat, in his
night-life dreams, he places himself first of all at the center of
the family and then he places the family in the heavens where
he and they rule the universe above and the world below. It is
useful to note that in a "tilted family" a sense of uniqueness of
the family is typically developed and maintained.[9]

The compensatory aspect of this dream is akin to the dream
that Jung reports in which he was looking up from the ground
level to a woman patient on a balcony above. He realized he had
been "looking down" on her and the dream told him to redress
the balance. He commented that the therapy went fine after that.

Joseph's dream also reminds me of a male university student
who felt de-potentiated with the women he had dated during his
four years of study. In the last month of his final semester, he
dreamed that he gathered all of the women he had dated into one
room and told them off! The element of counter-phobic imagery is
present in his and in Joseph's dreams.

However, the most apparent characteristic of both of
Joseph's dreams is his narcissistic grandiosity. Clearly this trig-
gered the same thing in his brothers inasmuch as they were outraged by Joseph's relating his dreams to them.

3. Sanford refers to Kunkel's four types of egocentricity as:
(a) The Turtles, who find life so frightening that they pull inside
their shell and hide; (b) The Tyrants, who are so paranoid that
they protect themselves by controlling others; (c) The Clinging
Vines, who are over-dependent on others; (d) The Stars, who

seek to be on center stage so they can be admired by others. When an ego crisis occurs, that event provides the best hope for the process of individuation to begin. Frequently, however, the egocentric person will simply shift to another egocentric type.[10]

In the case of Joseph, his Clinging Vine *persona* is no longer working. In his dreams Joseph depicts himself as a Star. The danger is that he will become a Tyrant, as we shall see later.

4.   Now let us turn to three other figures in his dreams.

Benjamin. Since Joseph loved his only full-blooded brother, how does Benjamin come to be lumped in with the others? If we accept both the genuineness of Joseph's love for his only brother, but also accept the ambivalence in close human relationships, it is possible to discern elements other than love but present along side of it.

One important factor is that Benjamin displaced Joseph as the youngest, most privileged son in their father's eyes. Jealousy would be one very strong responsive emotion most likely to occur when the older brother's status is destroyed, especially in the face of the absence of the mother.

Furthermore, it would not be surprising for the displaced son to look at his younger brother, Benjamin, as the cause of their mother's death, with the emotional response being one of strong resentment at the cause of his loss and so of all of his woes. Jealousy, resentment, and some hatred could in turn evoke guilt for the negative emotions toward his loved and loving young brother who in turn evoked loving memories of his mother.

Rachel. Joseph's mother is also included in the second dream as bowing down to him. First of all, it is not without reason that spoiled, narcissistic boys in a patriarchal era are referred to as child-tyrants. Mothers are usually their primary means for narcissistic gratification.

Secondly, in the dream there is a strong wish fulfillment in the image of the resuscitation of Rachel together with an element of denial, for his mother is alive again. Not only is she alive, but she has returned to give the worship and adoration that Joseph needs to cover up his anxiety, pain, and the realistic sense of his vulnerability as a young adolescent.

Thirdly, there is the normal anger that a child would feel at the mother for her sudden abandonment of him through her sudden death, no matter what its cause.

Jacob. Finally, how is it that his father is submissively present in the second dream? At the birth of Benjamin, Joseph is no longer his father's favored, youngest son. So, at least in part, Joseph in his dream is expressing his rage, resentment, and aggression at his father for having displaced him from his favored status.

We could also speculate that Joseph's presence evokes Jacob's own grief at the loss of his beloved Rachel and so, subliminally, Jacob's own aggression is directed at Joseph. This is Joseph's unconscious use of "an eye for an eye and a tooth for a tooth" in having his father grovel before him.

Furthermore, we are reminded of Freud's comment that the youngest son in the family occupies a special position, often being the particular object of the mother's affection and of the father's jealousy. The youngest son is also, according to Freud, the one who is most likely to displace the father. That Jacob has an intuitive grasp of this truth is shown by the high degree of ambivalence Jacob shows to Joseph from the time of his birth. It is also sadly demonstrated by the events that immediately follow.

Before turning to these events and examining their psychological significance, it is worth observing that I have not dealt with the traditional, ancient way of using dreams as prophetic or predictive, even though the biblical redactor did this. Nor have I hurried to the archetypal symbolism of the mandala in the circle of sheaves. Also I have not dealt with the off-center nature of the mandala in the second dream where a star and not the sun is the center of the universe, even though this last piece of imagery could be seen as a warning in the second dream that something is seriously out of order in Joseph's seventeen-year-old life.

II. THE TRANSFORMATION OF JOSEPH

We shall now look briefly at the process which enabled a wounded, narcissistic youth to stand before Pharaoh, a mere 13 years later, interpreting the Pharaoh's dreams so confidently that he became the Governor of Egypt for at least fourteen years.

A. *Shortly after Joseph shared his dreams* this fearful yet arrogant seventeen-year-old suffered a double betrayal in his own family. The obvious betrayal, which is well known, was at the hands of his elder brothers. In the normal hierarchy and structure of families, the older, more experienced brothers are expected to protect the younger ones. In this case, their impulse to kill and to hide the murder parallels Esau's lethal intentions to his younger twin brother Jacob for stealing his father's blessing. It is worth noting that the brothers parallel Esau and that Joseph parallels his father at this point. We may wonder if Jacob had a subliminal sense of this parallelism.

However, instead of killing him the brothers sold Joseph as a slave to a passing caravan of Midianites; they in turn sold him to an Egyptian named Potiphar. Throughout this experience, Joseph is depicted as remaining silent. We can speculate that he was overwhelmed by the fear of death and the terror of annihilation, and later by the pain of loneliness and rejection. He also had to learn to speak and read Egyptian! This scarification or purification of the soul can only be appreciated in retrospect. There is nothing like betrayal to destroy the defenses of a rigid *persona* or to shatter a false self. Much later, Joseph, utilizing an Egyptian wisdom-tradition and shaping an early Hebrew wisdom style of interpretation, was able to reframe the brothers' hostile actions as the working of the providence of God on behalf of the whole family.

Returning to the immediacy of the experience, one can imagine that it must have been devastating for Joseph, as he lay incarcerated in the *pit*—the word which is used as a metaphor for Sheol—to experience the dawning recognition that it was his own father Jacob who sent him out unprotected and defenseless to face his hostile brothers. It is true that he wore his special coat as if it were a magical shield or a sort of teddy bear which he could clutch as a mother-protector-substitute.

But at some point in the pit (or snake pit, as it is sometimes translated) he must have come to the realization that, with Benjamin back at home safe with his father, and with himself about to be murdered by his own brothers, it was his own father who had broken the rule on which patriarchal families are founded, namely, that the head of the family, the father, secures safety and protection for all other members of the family.

In this flash of reality, Joseph had his narcissistic illusions shattered. In the pit, waiting for death, he now recognized with searing pain what he unconsciously suspected and what was implicit in his second dream, that his father loved him, but also subliminally resented and hated him, even to the point of wanting him eliminated.[11] With the removal of his special coat, the protection of his narcissistic grandiosity is symbolically destroyed.

B. *Paradoxically, the construction of a true Self* begins for the young man Joseph as a slave in Egypt. Potiphar, the Pharaoh's chief security officer, gave Joseph increasing levels of responsibility. Finding himself trusted, Joseph began to trust himself in a new adult fashion and the mature character began to build. Thus, Potiphar incarnates a good father for Joseph. Egypt becomes a new motherland. So the bad father who betrayed him and the bad mother who abandoned him are replaced by new outer and inner objects or images which nurture and are nurtured.

C. *The second testing of Joseph occurred* when he heroically withstood the attempted seduction by Potiphar's wife but landed in jail as the victim of innocent suffering. Joseph withstood temptation and endured his imprisonment with a sense of loyalty to the good father and with a sense of ethical responsibility derived from a strong, protective superego. Strengthened by this transformation of his earlier, infantile narcissism he was able to give encouragement and leadership, through a growing belief in the providence of God, for the years of his incarceration in Pharaoh's prison (much like leadership given by a few a in P.O.W. camp).

III. JOSEPH, THE DREAM INTERPRETER

A. *Jail Dreams.* The next step in Joseph's maturation comes through his encounter in jail with Pharaoh's chief cup bearer (the chief butler) and chief baker. Recognizing Joseph's ability to take responsibility, the captain of the guard entrusted them and other prisoners to Joseph's care. This captain, too, becomes another incarnation of a good father for Joseph, for he recognizes the son's true worth.

One morning, Joseph finds the two men downcast because they have each had a dream and there are no professional dream interpreters available to help them understand what they accurately sense are vital dreams. Confidently, Joseph offers to interpret their dreams since "interpretation belongs to [his] God."

> 9) So the chief butler told his dream to Joseph, and said to him, "In my dream there was a vine before me, 10) and on the vine there were three branches; as soon as it budded, its blossoms shot forth, and the clusters ripened into grapes. 11) Pharaoh's cup was in my hand; and I took the grapes and pressed them into Pharaoh's cup, and placed the cup in Pharaoh's hand." 12) Then Joseph said to him, "this is its interpretation: the three branches are three days; 13) within three days Pharaoh will lift up your head and restore you to your office; and you shall place Pharaoh's cup in his hand as formerly, when you were his butler. 14) But remember me, when it is well with you, and do me the kindness, I pray you, to make mention of me to Pharaoh, and so get me out of this house. 15) For I was indeed stolen out of the land of the Hebrews; and here also I have done nothing that they should put me into the dungeon." (Gen. 40:9–15)

We see that Joseph, along the lines of traditional Egyptian dream interpretation gave a prediction which was extremely positive to the chief cup bearer.

Seeing that the previous prediction was favorable, the chief baker asks Joseph to interpret his dream.

> 16) When the chief baker saw that the interpretation was favorable, he said to Joseph, "I also had a dream: there were three cake baskets on my head, 17) and in the uppermost basket there were all sorts of baked food for Pharaoh, but the birds were eating it out of the basket on my head." 18) And Joseph answered, "This is its interpretation: the three baskets are three days; 19) within three days Pharaoh will lift up your head—from you!—and hang you on a tree; and the birds will eat the flesh from you." (Gen. 40:16–19)

No reason is given in the text for the difference in the outcome of the two dreams. One Jungian interpreter argues that the cup bearer took risks while the baker only got involved after it seemed safe.[12]

Another way to approach the dreams would be to say that, in his dream, the chief cup bearer plays the role of the nourishing mother to Pharaoh. He acts as a personal wine-press for the grapes of Pharaoh in addition to being the taster and so the protector of Pharaoh as he gives his lord the wine to drink.

The chief baker, however, in his dream, is the object of the birds' aggression (as in the Hitchcock movie). He may be dealing with anxiety resulting from his own oral aggression. His execution then is a literalization of an attack by the punitive superego. As Zeligs puts it, "his dream may express a fear resulting from his own projected hostile wishes."[13]

B. *Pharaoh's Dreams.* Two years later, Pharaoh himself had two dreams which his professional dream interpreters could not explain. The chief cup bearer remembered Joseph, so he was cleaned up and taken to Pharaoh.

> 1) After two years, Pharaoh dreamed that he was standing by the Nile, 2) and behold, there came up out of the Nile seven cows sleek and fat, and they fed in the reed grass. 3) And behold, seven other cows, gaunt and thin, came up out of the Nile after them, and stood by the other cows on the bank of the Nile. 4) And the gaunt and thin cows ate up the seven sleek and fat cows. And Pharaoh awoke. 5) And he fell asleep and dreamed a second time; and behold, seven ears of grain, plump and good, were growing on one stalk. 6) And behold, after them sprouted seven ears, thin and blighted by the east wind. 7) And the thin ears swallowed up the seven plump and full ears. And Pharaoh awoke, and behold, it was a dream. (Gen. 41:1–7)

Again, Joseph is depicted as using the interpretive principle that dreams are predictive in symbolic form. For our purpose what is noteworthy is that Joseph now sees himself not as the center but as one who serves the one who rules. This suggests that the Joseph-ego is no longer inflated but becomes the servant of the Pharaoh-Self.

As a result, Joseph can carry the dream on and advocate a course of action to deal with the crisis of the next fourteen years. Pharaoh discerns in him "the man who is discrete and wise [the wisdom theme] and is to be set over the land of Egypt" (Gen. 41:8). Joseph is, so to say, appointed Minister of the Interior!

We may note that the three Egyptians (the chief cup bearer, the chief baker, and Pharaoh) all have oral themes in their dreams: drinking wine, eating bread and cake, grain eating grain and cows eating cows. Joseph's first dream of the sheaves in the field also fits the theme of orality with its imagery of grain and food. Orality is expressed in imagery of food; the corresponding psychological thematic is nurturance.

Several symbolic events have occurred simultaneously.

1. Pharaoh becomes a good father to Joseph. The national trust and responsibility placed on Joseph allow him to receive reaffirmation of his earlier steps in learning to trust himself.

2. The themes of wisdom and the providence of God begin to coalesce for Joseph.

3. Joseph, like the cupbearer, is placed at Pharaoh's side. The role of both is that of nurturing mother. In nurturing the people of Egypt, Joseph gives mothering to the people of Egypt, thus living out what he was deprived of after his mother died when he was about seven years old.

4. Not only is the good mother the land and people of Egypt, but the Nile River itself is the flowing of nourishment from the symbolic breast.

5. Joseph has found a home both literally and psychologically: the house of Pharaoh, the home of his wife and children, and a home country all coalesce in the imagery of finding himself at home.

C. *Joseph's Family Reunion.* With considerable drama and irony, the story continues to a moment where Joseph is surrounded by his brothers kneeling before him and begging—just as they did in his first dream.

Benjamin also is brought to Egypt and stands terrified before the Lord of this superpower. He is confused because he is given special treatment in the face of his elder brothers— just like his brother Joseph had been treated before him.

Finally, after causing his father immense anxiety over several years at the potential loss of two more of his sons (Simeon and Benjamin), Jacob is under the sway of his own son. With Benjamin standing for the presence of the beloved mother, Joseph stands at the center of his family, ruling the "universe" of Egypt, which is the concretization of the fantasy of the tilted family and of the dream of the great star.

However, the enactment of the final scene differs in significant ways from the dream of the seventeen-year-old Joseph.

First of all, he is now strong enough to break down and cry unrestrainedly with the very brothers who abused him. He let himself be vulnerable to them, but was not destroyed by them.

Second, instead of egocentric centrality, Joseph depicts himself as one chosen by God's providence to go ahead and prepare for the salvation of his family, giving them the nurturing and protection that they did not give him.

That the brothers saw themselves as protected from their brother, the lord of Egypt, by their father's ambivalent love for Joseph is demonstrated after his death. They fear that Joseph will now seek revenge. Joseph has matured, but they have not changed and so they cannot grasp his capacity to forgive or how much he longs for their fraternal love. Joseph's infantile narcissism has undergone a radical transformation.

IV. CONCLUDING AMBIGUOUS POSTSCRIPT

A. *Regression and Aging.* Jung argued that age forty marks a turning point for spiritual maturation. But studies of Martin Luther by Erik Erikson, Roland Bainton, and Gordon Rupp have shown there is equally a capacity for regression.

1. *Jacob.* Jacob's neurotic preference for the younger son continues throughout his life: in this respect he justifies his presence in Joseph's second dream.

First of all, Jacob excludes Joseph from being immortalized by having his name attached to one of the tribes of Israel. Jacob virtually takes possession of Joseph's two Egyptian-born sons. But in elevating them while excluding Joseph, he deprives Joseph of honor just as he deprived his brother Esau of their Father's blessing.

Furthermore, when Joseph does present the elder son for Jacob's blessing, Jacob, in one of the final acts of his life, refuses him and blesses the younger one first against Joseph's protestations. Dorothy Zeligs suggests that Jacob is punishing Joseph for daring to rise above his father in power and status.[14]

Thus Jacob, at the very end of his life, denies his son the status of adult male and treats him still as a son. Nevertheless, the dutiful son does embalm his dead father and places him in a casket—probably one of those great anthropoid caskets—and buries him in the cave of Machpelah with his ancestors

Abraham, Sarah, Isaac, Rebekah and Leah. The beloved Rachel is left buried on the road between Bethlehem and Jerusalem. We wonder what made Joseph not place his mother with his father.

2. *Joseph.* In reflecting on Joseph's second dream, reference was made to the "star" quality of Joseph's egocentric self- imagery. We also observed that in Kunkel's typology a star could become a tyrant wielding power as a corrupt form of leadership. Regrettably something of this nature did occur during the years of famine.

When at first there was no bread in the land due to the famine, Joseph gathered the people's money in exchange for food. Then, when there was neither food nor money, Joseph took their cattle in exchange for food. Next he took their lands into state ownership for food. Finally he took their bodies as slaves, in exchange for food. Only the lands of the priests were exempt. Joseph masterminded this land-grab in the midst of a depression.

Furthermore, the Hebrews received preferential treatment from him during this period of time and they "gained possessions and were fruitful and multiplied exceedingly." However, much the redactor intended this special treatment to glorify Joseph, the fact is that the sufferings of the people would have led them to regard this specially privileged group with great hostility and hatred. Thus the Hebrews, by being given a special place and privilege, were set up by Joseph for possible "anti- semitism."

The point is that Joseph repeated his own early upbringing and so paved the way for the predictable result. In fact, the enslavement of the Hebrews by a Pharaoh "who knew not Joseph" (Exod. 1:8) may have merely been his legitimation of the envious wrath of the dispossessed people of Egypt. If so, there is a parallel here to the way in which Jacob tacitly legitimated the brothers' aggression against the special treatment given to Joseph. Joseph had set his people up for a tragic repetition of his own disaster at seventeen years of age.

It is possible to look at the dreams of the chief cup bearer and the chief baker as the good and bad aspects of Joseph's own shadow. While the chief cup bearer aspect of Joseph's ego is lifted up to Pharaoh (the Self), the chief baker aspect of Joseph's ego is in danger of being impaled for his tyrannical narcissism. Regression is as possible after the age of forty, as is personal growth toward maturity.

B. *Ancient Egyptian Wisdom and the Joseph Narrative.* Von Rad and others have emphasized the accuracy of information given about Egyptian life and customs in the Joseph narrative.[15] To this he adds the possible coalition of Egyptian and early Hebrew Wisdom, that is, in the Wisdom of Amenemope, the ideal wise man is described as discrete, moderate, self-controlled, and deliberate—which are also characteristics of Joseph in the surrounding narratives. Joseph is an administrator who gives good counsel, speaks well at the decisive moment, and gives sound advice in matters of state.

Furthermore, the Egyptian Amenemope writes: "That which man purposes is nothing; what God purposes is another thing."[16] This sense of the providence of God is also found in Joseph when he says to his brothers, "You meant evil against me, but God meant it for good."

The Wisdom of Amenemope also speaks about God "controlling events so that what is incomprehensible to man, suits the divine plan." Joseph is, in the Egyptian perspective, a man of wisdom. Von Rad believes that this is consonant with an early view of Hebrew Wisdom.[17]

We could add from a psychological perspective that Joseph's wisdom is also centered in his ability to be responsive to God's interpretation of dreams. This is a key source of wisdom for him as it had been for his father and great-grandfather.

❋ 3 ❋

Johannine Symbolism

MICHAEL WILLETT NEWHEART

The symbol which shines brightest in the Gospel of John is that of light. Indeed, it appears in the opening section of the Gospel: "In the beginning was the Word. . . . In him was light, and that light was the light of humanity. The light shines in the darkness, and the darkness has not overcome it" (John 1:1, 4–5). This language alludes to the opening verses of Genesis, where in the beginning of creation God says, "Let there be light!" thus separating light and darkness (Gen. 1:1, 3–4). In this essay I will attempt to allow some light to shine on the dark, mysterious yet attractive subject of Johannine symbolism. In order to do so, I will first survey recent developments in the interpretation of Johannine symbolism. I will then suggest how psychology might be useful in the interpretation of the symbols. Next I will discuss the approach to symbols used by the analytical psychology of C. G. Jung. Finally, I will sketch a Jungian reading of the Johannine symbols.

Preliminary to the task, though, are a few definitions. "Johannine symbolism" refers to the symbolism in the Gospel of John, which is also referred to as "the Fourth Gospel" or, in this essay, simply "the Gospel." It is distinguished from the Synoptic Gospels, which consist of Matthew, Mark, and Luke. The Epistles of John are considered only in a side glance, and the Revelation of John is not considered at all. The "Johannine community" refers to the group of Christians from which came the documents known as the Gospel and Epistles of John. "The evangelist" or "the Fourth Evangelist" refers to the author of the Gospel of John; no further attempt at an identification will be made.

I. Recent Discussion of Johannine Symbolism

Johannine symbolism has been a subject of considerable interest among New Testament scholars in the last decade or so. Indeed, their concerns reflect those of biblical critics at large. In this first section of the essay, then, I will discuss recent studies of Johannine symbolism, especially those of a historical or literary nature, and then I will offer a critique from a psychological perspective.

From the Enlightenment until very recently, critical biblical scholarship has been dominated by historical interests, so that the reigning paradigm has been historical criticism. These historical interests have been evident in treatments of Johannine symbolism. For example, in the 1980 presidential address to the Society for New Testament Studies, Xavier Leon-Dufour attempted a "symbolic reading" of the Fourth Gospel which was thoroughly grounded in history.[1] The word "symbol" literally means "put together," and he attempted to "put together" the surface meaning of the symbols in the Gospel text and the deeper reality to which they point. The "symbolic operation," then, sets up an "analogical relationship" between two realities, which in the Fourth Gospel are the Jewish cultural milieu in which Jesus lived and the Christian cultural milieu in which the evangelist wrote.[2] A symbolic reading "discovers the relationship between the present reality of the Spirit and the times past of Jesus of Nazareth."[3]

New Testament scholars, though, have never been satisfied with just history; they have always sought to supplement their historical investigations with tools from other disciplines. For example, Rudolf Bultmann, the premier New Testament scholar of this century, used the existentialist philosophy of Martin Heidegger in order to interpret the biblical text. In his monumental commentary on the Fourth Gospel he wrote that light is the "illumined condition of existence, of my own existence."[4] This existentialist approach to Johannine symbolism was continued by John Painter.[5] The symbols, he wrote, are objects from this world but "point beyond this realm to that which makes human existence authentic."[6] Painter also attempted to set the symbols in the context of the conflict between the Johannine community and the synagogue. The evangelist held that synagogue Jews had a "false understanding of the symbols," while believers in his community had "the new authentic understanding" in Jesus.[7] The evangelist took symbols which synagogue Jews would have understood in terms of the Jewish Law and gave them a new point of reference in Jesus.

In the last decade or so, however, the existentialist approach has been criticized because it interprets history as a history of ideas of the early church and neglects concrete social settings out of which the texts emerged. New Testament scholars, therefore, have turned to the social sciences in order to help explicate the social milieu of first-century Christianity.[8] Robin Scroggs noted that the use of social sciences in the study of the New Testament is an attempt to "put body and soul together again."[9] Studies using a social-scientific approach to Johannine symbolism have focused on the social function of the symbols. For example, George MacRae noted that many of the symbols in the Fourth Gospel were paralleled in the Hellenistic literature of the day. He suggested that the evangelist incorporated a diversity of symbols in the Gospel in order to emphasize the universality of Jesus.[10] On the other hand, Wayne Meeks maintained that the images in the Gospel depicted Jesus as an alien in this world in order to give legitimacy to the Johannine community of Christians who, because of their separation from their Jewish origins, felt alienated from society at large.[11] Craig Koester, however, emphasized both the universality and the particularity of Johannine symbolism. Koester contended that the symbols strengthened the community's distinct social identity by evoking various associations in the minds of the Jews, Gentiles, and Samaritans who made up the Johannine community. Yet the symbols were transformed christologically so that Jesus himself became the unifying center of the community.[12]

New Testament scholarship in general, and studies of Johannine symbolism in particular, have been dominated by historical concerns, clarified in recent years by social-science perspectives. Another important recent movement, however, has focused on literary concerns, that is, an emphasis on the text itself rather than the community or social milieu out of which the text came. The difference between historical criticism and literary criticism in New Testament scholarship is often phrased in terms of "window and mirror." Historical critics see the text as a "window" through which they can view the early Christian community and the world in which it lived. Literary critics, however, view the text as a "mirror" in which readers can "see" the world in which they live. Meaning is found in the interaction between text and reader.[13]

Biblical literary critics have principally employed in their investigations narrative criticism and reader-response theory.[14] Alan Culpepper discussed Johannine symbolism in his major study of the Fourth Gospel from a narrative-critical perspective. His section on symbols appears in the chapter on implicit commentary.[15] Culpepper maintained that any treatment of Johannine symbolism must be based on adequate definitions, be sensitive to movement and development in the Gospel, must relate the metaphors, symbols, and motifs to one another, and analyze their function within the Gospel as a literary whole.[16] He then focused on "core symbols" or "expanding symbols," such as light, water, and bread, which serve by repetition balanced by variation, and this variation progressively discloses to us a sphere which is of great concern.[17] Robert Kysar looked at Johannine metaphors using reader-response criticism.[18] He contended that the reader's experience of the metaphors is affective as well as cognitive, for they elicit "emotional instability" for the reader.[19] Kysar also talked about the metaphors' "participatory feature," "shock," and "decisional character."[20]

Recent works in Johannine symbolism have been dominated by historical and literary concerns. Yet, it seems that studies from both perspectives have been unconsciously groaning and straining toward a psychological perspective. For example, Painter's existentialist-historical study said that the symbols "point beyond this realm to that which makes human existence authentic." From a literary standpoint, Culpepper wrote that the core symbols in the Gospel disclose a sphere which is of great concern. Depth psychologists would add that the realm "which makes human existence authentic" or the "sphere which is of great concern" is the unconscious, and that symbols serve as mediators between consciousness and the unconscious. Meeks, looking at the symbols from a social-historical perspective, spoke of how the Gospel's symbolic universe helped the Johannine community deal with the alienation which it felt from society at large. Yet alienation is a psychological as well as a social phenomenon; it wounds the psyche of group members and it allows the individual to separate from the collective and move toward wholeness. How did the symbols in the Fourth Gospel help the Johannine community members do this? Social history, therefore, must be supplemented by psychological history. Koester seemed to be taking an unwitting step in this direction when he wrote that the Gospel's symbols evoked various associations in the minds of the Jews, Gentiles, and Samaritans who made up the Johannine community. What kind of associations were evoked, and why were they evoked at all? Might one say that these symbols arose out of the collective unconscious, and their use in the Fourth Gospel activated the archetypes in the minds of the readers or listeners?

Reader-response criticism also seems to be knocking on the door of psychology. Kysar spoke about the reader's "affective" experience of the metaphors in the Fourth Gospel and the "emotional instability" they elicit. What is the nature of this affective experience and this emotional instability? Is it not the metaphors bringing unconscious issues into the reader's consciousness? Writing in the same volume on literary approaches to the Fourth Gospel in which Kysar's essay appears, Wilhelm Wuellner called for the rehabilitation of psychological exegesis to supplement the new literary approaches.[21] Stephen Moore, in his book on the use of literary criticism in the study of the Gospels, charged that New Testament reader-critics' readings were "ineluctably cerebral" and "emotionally retarded."[22] Indeed, I think that such readings are the result of the insensitivity biblical literary critics have to the unconscious issues which the symbols raise in the reading experience. I might go so far as to suggest that critics' "ineluctably cerebral" readings are a defense against the unconscious issues which the symbols raise for them. Perhaps depth psychology can help "emotionally retarded" biblical scholars recover their feeling function.

II. THE RELEVANCE OF PSYCHOLOGY

It is time, therefore, for psychology to take its rightful place alongside historical and literary criticism in the study of biblical texts, and specifically Johannine symbols. This second section of the essay will briefly discuss the kinds of questions psychology raises for the study of the New Testament in general and Johannine symbolism in particular, and then it will note recent studies by New Testament scholars which have used psychological approaches, especially Jungian approaches.

Psychology has much to add to both historical and literary perspectives; it can illuminate what we see through the window and in the mirror of the text, that is, it can help us to understand the mind of the person and the community which produced the text, and it can help us plumb the mind of contemporary readers as they encounter the text. Psychology is after all "the study of the soul" (*psyche* + *logos*), and of what does the New Testament consist but "soul books," written by, about, and for persons who, through their relationship with the Ultimate, were transformed in the depths of their being? Psychology can help us analyze these transformations in behavior, in feeling, and in relationship.[23] Indeed, it was noted above that other social sciences are said to help keep "body and soul" together, with social structures identified as the body and ideology as the soul. Would it not be more appropriate, however, to consider ideology as mind and psyche as soul? Psychology works alongside social sciences and literary criticism in the investigation of New Testament texts to keep body, mind, and soul together.

Indeed, psychology raises a whole host of questions for the interpreter to ask of New Testament texts in general and of Johannine symbolism in particular. Not only must one ask about the historical, existential, social, and narrative function of the Johannine symbols, one also needs to ask: What is the psychological function of these symbols? How did they function in the psyche of the first-century Johannine Christian, and how do they function in the psyche of the twentieth-century reader? Whether we look at the Fourth Gospel as a window or as a mirror, the symbols must be considered psychologically in order to get a full perspective.

In the last ten years two major works have been produced by New Testament scholars which utilize psychological approaches. Indeed, they represent two different ways to use psychology in New Testament studies. The first of these works was Gerd Theissen's *Psychological Aspects of Pauline Theology*. Theissen is perhaps best known for his pioneering work in the social-scientific study of the New Testament, but in this book he broke new ground in the psychological study. His definition of psychological exegesis was particularly instructive: it "seeks to describe and explain, as far as possible, human behavior and experience in ancient Christianity. . . . Under the rubric of psychological exegesis, we include all attempts to interpret texts as expression and occurrence of human experience and behavior."[24] For Theissen, psychological exegesis allowed the text to serve as a "window" onto the psyche of the first-century Christian. To this end, he gave attention to behavioral, cognitive, and psychodynamic perspectives.

The second important work in this area was Walter Wink's three-volume study of the Powers in the New Testament, in which he takes a psychological, as well as socio-ethical, approach to the Powers.[25] Even before the appearance of this work, however, Wink began to make a case for the use of psychology in biblical study. In his controversial 1973 tract *The Bible in Human Transformation*, Wink wrote that historical biblical criticism was "bankrupt" of possibilities for personal and social transformation, and he turned to psychology to restore its solvency.[26] For Wink, psychology allowed the New Testament text to serve as a "mirror" onto the reader's psyche. In an article on utilizing psychological insights in biblical study, he wrote, "We have analyzed the text; now we may wish to find ways to let it analyze us."[27]

Both Theissen and Wink used the analytical psychology of C. G. Jung in their work. For Theissen, Jung was one of several psychologists whose methods he used. Wink's early work in the psychological study of the New Testament was almost exclusively Jungian, but his more recent work on the powers has supplemented that emphasis with the work of social psychologists. Other biblical scholars have employed Jung in their investigations. Wayne Rollins has written extensively on the relevance of Jungian psychology for the interpretation of the

Bible.[28] Schuyler Brown has produced Jungian analyses of aspects of the Gospels of Matthew and John,[29] and I have written on Jung and John.[30]

Psychology has some important perspectives to bring to bear on the New Testament text in general and Johannine symbolism in particular. Some New Testament scholars are beginning to recognize this potential and are beginning to use psychological insights. Indeed, a number are looking to the work of Jung.

EXCURSUS ON DIEL, SYMBOLISM IN THE FOURTH GOSPEL

Before looking at Jung, however, it seems appropriate to comment on a book which seemingly does what this paper is seeking to do, that is, to give a psychological analysis of Johannine symbols. Written by psychologist Paul Diel, the book is entitled *Symbolism in the Gospel of John*.[31] Unfortunately, it is a model of how not to do psychological analyses of biblical texts! First, the book contains no dialogue with either biblical critics or other psychologists. Diel maintained that biblical critics pursue "dogmatic exegesis," which is concerned with supporting the dogmas of the church.[32] (Such a statement betrays an amazing ignorance of the history of modern biblical criticism, which is littered with controversy between the church and biblical scholars.)[33] Diel's lack of dialogue with other psychologists is particularly curious, for his work is similar in many ways to that of Freud and Jung. (The back cover of the book identifies Diel as a "post-Jungian.") Furthermore, Diel was plagued by an ahistorical bias. He wrote in one place, "It is really not that important whether Jesus actually lived or not."[34] And in his interpretation of the prologue he said, "God does not exist, the Word does not exist, the beginning does not exist, Christ is not a person, spirit and flesh are not entities. All these words are only symbols, 'figures of speech.'"[35] As a result he engaged in a kind of allegorical interpretation using his own idiosyncratic "Psychology of Motivation." For example, in interpreting John 1:48–51, Nathanael's initial encounter with Jesus, Diel wrote that the fig tree symbolizes the "vital impulse," the open sky represents "inner joy," and the angels are Jesus' superconscious.[36] Such allegorization reduces the Gospel's evocative symbols to signs which have a one-to-one correspondence with their meaning. Additionally, such an approach does not consider the literary function of the symbols within the Gospel narrative itself nor does it attempt to locate the symbols in the cultural milieu of the Johannine community. Any reading of the symbols in the Fourth Gospel, whether it be sociological, narratological, or psychological, must respect the Gospel text itself and the milieu which gave it birth.

III. JUNG'S APPROACH TO SYMBOLS

The analytical psychology of C. G. Jung has much to add to the study of Johannine symbolism, for the study of myth and symbol was at the heart of his work. Indeed, the book which led to Jung's break with Sigmund Freud was entitled *Symbols of Transformation*,[37] and his last book, which he edited, was called *Man and His Symbols*.[38] This section will briefly summarize Jung's approach to symbols, looking at his function of symbols in the psyche and their appearance in dreams and in art and literature.

In order for a person to move to maturity, or what Jung called "individuation," one must bring consciousness into dialogue with the unconscious. These opposites can be brought together only through symbols, which arise spontaneously out of the unconscious and are amplified through the conscious mind.[39] Symbols have a uniting quality.[40] They unite opposites within the psyche, such as the conscious and the unconscious. Jung called this uniting function of symbols their "transcendent function."[41]

Jung distinguished sharply between signs and symbols. Signs are invented and are thus products of the conscious mind. Jung used the example of abbreviations such as UN or NATO. Symbols, however, are not invented, but they arise out of the unconscious and thus have numinous power. Jung wrote, "A sign is always less than the thing it points to, and a symbol is always more than we can understand at first. Therefore, we never stop at the sign but go on to the goal it indicates; but we remain with the symbol because it promises more than it reveals."[42]

Symbols are formed by certain tendencies or patterns in the collective unconscious which Jung called "archetypes."[43] Archetypes include the shadow, anima/animus, and the Self. The shadow is the sum total of what one refuses to acknowledge about oneself.[44] Anima is the feminine principle in the male, and animus is the masculine principle in the female.[45] The Self facilitates the reconciliation between the conscious and unconscious.[46] It is the archetype of wholeness, the ordering and unifying center of the psyche, what Jung called the "God-image" within us.[47]

Jung believed that dreams were the chief source of all our knowledge about symbolism.[48] Dream analysis held an important place in Jung's approach to symbols. He pursued a twofold approach in interpreting dream symbols: association and amplification. First, he encouraged the dreamer to list all the personal associations which a symbol evoked for him or her. Second, Jung "amplified" the symbol by bringing to bear the various meanings which the symbol carried in religious traditions, mythologies, folklore, and fairy tales. Interpretation of the dream symbol was done at both the personal and general levels. Jung also often had the dreamer respond to the symbol in a personal way, such as fantasy, art, drama, or poetry, in a process known as "active imagination."[49]

In all his work with dream symbolism, Jung always led the dreamer back to the dream itself. He believed that only the material that was clearly and visibly part of the dream should be used in interpreting it. For example, Jung distinguished sharply his method of dream interpretation from Sigmund Freud's method, known as "free association," in which the dreamer made a chain of associations, and one association led to another. For Jung, however, the dreamer was to return continually to the symbol itself in order to make associations. While he compared free association with a "zigzag line" which leads away from the dream itself, Jung compared his method to "a circumambulation, the centre of which is the dream-image."[50] Jung, therefore, paid close attention to both the form and content of the dream. He was fond of telling his students, "Learn as much as you can about symbolism; then forget it all when you are analyzing a dream."[51]

Jung maintained that the general function of dreams was to restore psychological balance. The psyche is a self-regulating system, he said, which reestablishes psychic equilibrium through dream material. Dreams, therefore, have a complementary or compensatory function.[52] Jung viewed this idea of compensation as a "law of psychic happening," and when he set out to interpret a dream, he always asked: What conscious attitude does this dream compensate?[53]

Jung's approach to art and literature paralleled his approach to dreams, for he believed that the human psyche not only produced dreams, but it also was "the womb of all sciences and art."[54] Jung contended that there were two modes of artistic creation: the psychological and the visionary. The psychological mode deals with materials drawn from the realm of human consciousness, such as romance novels, murder mysteries, didactic poetry, and tragic and comic drama. The visionary mode, however, arises from the collective unconscious; it expresses the "primordial vision," that is, "true symbolic expression." Examples which Jung cited include Dante, William Blake's paintings and poetry, and Richard Wagner's operas.[55] Literature in the visionary mode is, like dreams, compensatory to the conscious attitude of the artist or author. Jung described theater as "an institution for working out private complexes in public."[56] Art and literature, however, also exercise a compensatory function for people of the day. Jung wrote, "Whenever the collective unconscious becomes a living experience and is brought to bear upon the conscious outlook of an age, this event is a creative act which is of importance to everyone living in that age. A work of art is produced that contains what may truthfully be called a message to generations of [people]."[57]

Symbols held an important place in the work of C. G. Jung. They perform a transcendent function in the psyche, uniting conscious and unconscious. Jung's approach to dream analysis gave significant attention to the symbols in the dreams, using association and amplification in order to bring the meaning of the symbol to light. Just as symbols in dreams perform a compensatory function in the psyche of the dreamer, symbols in art and literature perform a compensatory function in the individual psyche of the artist or author and in the collective psyche of people of that day.

IV. JOHANNINE SYMBOLISM IN JUNGIAN PERSPECTIVE

With all this in mind, how can one read Johannine symbolism from a Jungian perspective, informed by various historical and literary approaches? The final section of this chapter will sketch the broad outline of such a reading. I will first give attention to the Johannine symbolic universe, with its dualistic nature and its symbols of the Self, anima/animus, and shadow. Then I will try to locate the symbols in the experience of the Johannine community and evaluate them in terms of the experience of readers today.

The Johannine symbolic universe is dualistic in nature for it is dominated by opposites, such as light and darkness, spirit and flesh, life and death. Scholars, therefore, speak of the "Johannine dualism."[58] The primary dualism in the Gospel, however, is spatial, the dualism between the world above and the world below (cf. 3:31; 8:23). Jesus has come into this world from above in order that people might believe in him and be born from above (cf. 1:1–18; 3:1–21). The symbols are phenomena in this world which point to the world above, so that those in this world might, like Jesus, have their point of origin in the world above. The symbols bring together the world above and the world below. In Jungian language, the world above is the world within, the unconscious, while the world below is the outer world of ego-consciousness.[59] The symbols enter consciousness from the unconscious; they are manifested in the world below, but they come from the world above. They are expressed in terms of consciousness, but they point beyond themselves to the unconscious, so that the two may be integrated and the individual might experience wholeness. John Painter said it well in his existentialist interpretation of the symbols: "The symbols, derived from the world of sense experience, are used to communicate that which transcends the world in order that the transcendent might be experienced."[60] The transcendent becomes immanent, eternal life is *experienced* in this life, unconscious is made conscious as the opposites are reconciled in the human psyche. Thus, the Johannine symbols exercise their transcendent function, and they become symbols of transformation.

The symbols of transformation in the Gospel include water (4:10–15; 7:38), bread (6:35–58), and light (8:12; 9:5), but the central symbol, the symbol of the Self, the organizing principle of the psyche, is Jesus himself.[61] In no other Gospel does Jesus dominate the narrative as he does in the Fourth Gospel. He is the Word become flesh who comes down from above to work miracles and to speak in long discourses, and he returns to the world above through death, resurrection, and ascension. His miracles are not just altruistic deeds but "signs" that reveal Jesus' glory and indicate that he is from above (2:11). These signs—turning water into wine (2:1–11), healing a man born blind (9:1–7), raising Lazarus from the dead (11:1–44), dying, rising, and ascending (chaps. 18–21)—indicate that Jesus is a numinous figure, a messenger from above, or psychologically, a figure from the unconscious.

The discourses of Jesus in the Fourth Gospel differ significantly from his teaching in the Synoptic Gospels in which he teaches about the reign of God through parables. In the Fourth Gospel, the subject of the discourses is Jesus himself and the revelation he brings. Jesus points to himself through "I am" sayings, such as "I am the light of the world" (8:12); "I am the resurrection and the life" (11:25); and "Before Abraham was, I am" (8:58). Jesus' "I am" is the "I" of the Self breaking into consciousness, summoning persons to relationship with him. In order to interpret this "I," the central symbol Jesus takes various other symbols such as light, bread, vine, and shepherd and identifies himself with those. Through the "I am" sayings, the symbols are concentrated in Jesus, so they derive their energy from this symbol of the Self.

In discussing a social historical approach to the Johannine symbols, it was noted above that Koester maintained that the symbols unified the Johannine community because they evoked associations within the minds of the various community members. To use Jungian language, these symbols were performing a "transcendent function" in the psyche of community members before they entered the community, and when the symbols were applied to Christ they were brought under the power of the new symbol of the Self, Jesus. To take an example which Koester used, the image of the shepherd was familiar from Hebrew Scripture and Hellenistic writings as a symbol for leaders, both human and divine, who ruled, protected, and cared for the people. The father, the masculine principle, is projected onto an external figure. The human or divine leader becomes that father figure who cares for the individual like a child. In the Fourth Gospel Jesus says, "I am the good shepherd. The good shepherd lays down his life for the sheep. . . . I know my own and my own know me" (10:11, 14). Jesus is that nurturing father figure, even to the point of death. The symbol of the shepherd comes under the sway of the symbol of the Self, so that Jesus is defined as the nurturing Self and the shepherd is now defined in Jesus.

A Jungian reading of the Johannine symbols, therefore, surveys the appearance of symbols in the literature of the ancient Mediterranean world. This process is very similar to the method of dream interpretation which Jung called "amplification." When a particular symbol in the Gospel is considered, it is important to understand how that symbol functioned in the literature of the day, both Jewish and Hellenistic, not in order to try to prove some sort of dependence, as was the tendency of previous generations of scholars, but in order to understand the first-century psyche and the role the symbols played within that psyche. For example, in another "I am" saying, Jesus says, "I am the bread of life" (6:35, 48). To those from a Jewish background the symbol of bread would have evoked numerous associations: the Passover meal which celebrated the liberation from slavery in Egypt, the manna which God gave the Israelites as they wandered in the wilderness after liberation, the bread which Lady Wisdom served to those who would submit to her instruction, and finally the Law, which was symbolized as bread by the rabbis. So the symbol of bread was a feminine symbol which spoke of the nourishment which God provides to the people, the nourishment which the Self supplies to consciousness from the unconscious. When Jesus says that he is the bread of life, the bread that comes down from heaven, he becomes that nourishment from the unconscious. Furthermore, this image is also associated with death, for Jesus says that the bread that he gives is his flesh (6:51). The symbol of the Self redefines and is redefined by another symbol, so that the transforming function of the symbol of bread is now applied to Christ.

It is important to note that both of these symbols, shepherd and bread, are connected in the Fourth Gospel with death: Jesus is the good shepherd because he lays down his life for his flock, and is the bread of life in that he gives his flesh for the life of the world. The defining symbol of the symbol of the Self is the cross. The Johannine view of Jesus' death, however, is different from the Synoptics and Paul, for in the Fourth Gospel the cross is a lifting up and glorification (3:14; 8:28; 12:23, 32; 13:31–32; 17:1, 5); it is the way in which Jesus returns to God (7:33; 14:12, 28; 16:5, 9, 16). Death, resurrection, and ascension are not separated as they are in other New Testament works, but together they form one "hour," the hour of Jesus' exaltation. The cross thus casts its shadow over all the other symbols. All the other symbols are killed, crucified between the opposites. But it is only then that they, like Jesus, are glorified. Only through association with death are the symbols given numinous power, returning to the unconscious from which they came.

In the Fourth Gospel, therefore, Jesus is the symbol of the Self, and that symbol is interpreted by other symbols in the "I am" sayings. Other personal symbols appear in the narrative in the form of various male and female characters, that is, anima/animus figures. The male characters have the determinative roles in the Gospel: Peter confesses Jesus as the Holy One of God (6:69), later denies him (18:15–18, 25–27), but is given the task of shepherding the flock after Jesus' return to God (21:15–19); the beloved disciple has an intimate relationship with Jesus (13:23) and is the authoritative witness behind the Gospel (19:35; 21:24); Thomas initially refuses to believe reports of the resurrection but then confesses the Risen Jesus as Lord and God (20:24–29); and John the Baptist serves as witness to Jesus (1:6–8, 15, 29–35).

Female characters have important roles as well: the Samaritan woman brings her entire village to faith in Jesus (4:7–42); Martha confesses Jesus as the Christ, the Son of God (11:27); Mary anoints Jesus (12:3); and Mary Magdalene is the first to see the empty tomb and the Risen Jesus (20:11–18). At points in the narrative, the actions of women surpass those of men, for the story of the Samaritan woman is told immediately after the story of the misunderstanding Nicodemus (3:1–21), and the confession of Martha is greater than that of Peter.[62] The masculine principle is dominant in the narrative, but the feminine also has an important place. One might say that the narrative is "animus-driven," but the anima still has a place.

Nevertheless, all the characters, both male and female are defined by their responses to Jesus, whether those responses are misunderstanding or commitment.[63] The anima and animus figures are leading the reader toward the symbol of the Self.

In addition to symbols of the Self and anima/animus, shadow figures also appear in the Gospel, such as Satan, Judas, and Pilate. The darkest shadow, however, falls on a collective character, the Jews. No distinction is made between Pharisees, scribes, chief priests, and Sadducees, as in the Synoptics, but all these groups are collapsed into "the Jews." They are the primary enemies of Jesus: they continually debate with him (2:18–20; 5:16–18), and they seek to kill him (5:18; 7:1). The Jews are in conflict with Jesus because they are blind (9:40–41); their allegiance is to Caesar rather than God (19:15); they are children of the devil (8:44).[64] In other words, the Jews are oriented completely to this world, the world of ego-consciousness, and they struggle against Jesus, who is the messenger from the unconscious. Therefore, Jesus, the symbol of the Self, is clothed in pure light, while the Jews, the shadow figures, are painted in the darkest of colors.

The symbolic world of the Fourth Gospel, therefore, is dualistic in nature and consists of Jesus the symbol of the Self, who defines himself further through various symbols such as water, light, and bread; various anima/animus figures such as Peter, the beloved disciple, the mother of Jesus, and Mary Magdalene; and the shadow figures, principally the Jews. The question, however, arises: What "compensatory function" were these symbols exercising within the Johannine community when the Gospel was written? Jung said that works of literature, like dreams, perform a compensatory function in the psyche of the author and the people of that day. What attitude, then, was this Gospel compensating? The Gospel text seems to indicate that community members had recently experienced expulsion from the Jewish community. The community's situation appears to be symbolized in the experience of the blind man who, after being healed by Jesus, is put out of the synagogue by the Jewish authorities (9:1–41). Furthermore, secret believers in Jesus are afraid to make their faith public for fear they too might be expelled (12:42; cf. also 9:22). Jesus tells his disciples that after his death they will be put out of the synagogue (16:2). These references in the Gospel to being put out of the synagogue seem to reflect the situation of the Johannine community: originally a sect within Judaism, they had been expelled from the synagogue because of their confession that Jesus was the Messiah.[65]

David Rensberger summarized well the crisis the community would have experienced: "The Christians who were expelled would have been cut off from much that had given identity and structure to their lives. Expulsion would have meant social ostracism and thus the loss of relationship with family and friends, and perhaps economic dislocation as well. It would certainly have meant religious dislocation. The synagogue meetings, the public liturgy, the festivals, and the observances were all now denied them, and the authoritative interpretation of the sacred scripture itself was in the hands of their opponents. What was threatened was thus the entire universe of shared perceptions, assumptions, beliefs, ideals, and hopes that had given meaning to their world within Judaism."[66]

Through the Gospel narrative, the Johannine community was trying to maintain psychic equilibrium in the face of expulsion from the synagogue. The symbols in the Fourth Gospel were an important way in which they did this. The evangelist reclaimed symbols of transformation from the Jewish heritage, in which they referred to the Law, and refocused them on Jesus, so that the stabilizing effect which these symbols had were brought to bear upon their situation of crisis. The symbols provided psychic grounding for the Johannine Christians in the alienation which they felt from the synagogue. The living water, the bread of life, the light of the world was not found in the Law but in Jesus, the Johannine community's symbol of the Self.

It is particularly interesting to see the way that the evangelist uses the symbol of light and darkness. These symbols express perhaps better than any other the "Johannine dualism." Light is a universal symbol, representing truth, revelation, or consciousness. The Hebrew Scripture associated light with both Israel and the Law. Isaiah said that Israel was a light to the nations (49:6), and Psalm 119 said that the law was a lamp and a light (v. 105). This identification of the law and light was further elaborated by the rabbis, as the word "light" is occasionally replaced by "law."

For example, where Isaiah 2:5 reads, "Let us walk in the light of Yahweh," the Targum on it reads, "Let us walk in the study of the Law." First-century Judaism associated itself completely with light; it was the light and it had the light in the Law. In identifying itself so completely with light, though, it failed to deal with its own darkness. When one does not "own" one's darkness or shadow, it is projected onto others.[67] Synagogue authorities projected their shadow onto the Johannine Christians, who held a "deviant belief," that is, a new revelation of God in Jesus. The authorities held that they were in the light, and the Johannine Christians were in darkness. Therefore, the believers in Jesus were expelled from the synagogue, suppressed into the unconscious.

How were the Johannine Christians to cope with the trauma of expulsion, in which they were alienated from the collective, separated from the mother? In order to deal with this trauma, the community reversed the symbols of light and darkness. They maintained that they had the light in Jesus, but the synagogue authorities were in darkness because they had rejected Jesus by casting believers out of the community. The Johannine believers projected their own shadow onto the synagogue authorities. This projection is given shape in narratival form in the Gospel: the Jews, representing the synagogue authorities, are the shadow figures, while Jesus, standing for the Johannine community, is the light. The consciousness of the Johannine Christians, then, was split: they had the light of consciousness, but the synagogue authorities were totally in the darkness of the unconscious, the recipients of the community's projected shadow. Such projection was the only way the community could maintain psychic equilibrium in the aftermath of the trauma of expulsion.

Apparently the community's psyche remained split, for the Johannine epistles, written about a decade after the Fourth Gospel, indicate that the community itself eventually split. The author of the first epistle of John wrote concerning those who have left the community, "They went out from us, but they did not belong to us; for if they had belonged to us, they would have remained with us. But by going out they made it plain that none of them belongs to us" (1 John 2:19).[68] Some of the same language which the Gospel used for the Jews was now used for the members who left the community: they are in darkness (2:9–11), they are children of the devil (3:8), they are antichrists (2:18, 22; 4:3).

The split in consciousness was realized in the split in the body, that is, the social body, the Johannine community. After the split, the community seems to have disappeared. Those loyal to the author were integrated into the larger church, and those who had left the community found a place in Christian gnosticism.[69]

Up to this point we have been interpreting the Gospel as a "window" onto the psyche of the Johannine community as it struggled with life after expulsion from the synagogue. But the Gospel can also be approached as a "mirror" of the psyche of the modern reader. It is at this point that psychological criticism can join forces with some of the newer literary approaches, such as narrative criticism and reader-response criticism. The literary approaches note the participatory nature of the Johannine symbols. To use Jungian language, the symbols stir the depths of the human psyche because of their archetypal nature. One problem, however, with biblical reader-response criticism is that when the critic talks about the reader, it is really a reflection of the critic himself or herself! The reader is usually a white, male, well-educated, middle-class academic.[70] Such an approach does not respect the diversity of readers that encounter the text. Fernando Segovia has contended that biblical reader-response critics were not sufficiently critical of their social location, for a person's race, class, gender, religion, and politics will affect one's reading of the text.[71] Furthermore, one must be critical of one's psychological location as well. Unconscious issues will determine one's conscious reading of the text. Just as an author attempts to resolve complexes through writing a piece of literature, a reader attempts to resolve his or her own complexes through reading, especially when the reader considers that piece of literature scripture. The key question, then, is, How do the Johannine symbols function in the modern psyche?

Perhaps the answer depends on the reader's social and psychological location. What does the reader bring to the text? In order to determine that, perhaps the reader could describe associations that are stirred in the psyche by the Johannine symbols. Then the reader could utilize active imagination with the symbols. The Johannine symbols can still serve as symbols of transformation, in that the Gospel's dualistic symbolic structure vividly indicates that there is another world besides this world, another realm other than ego-consciousness. There is the world above or the unconscious, and that realm reveals itself to us and confronts us for a response. The Gospel can lead to transformation those who are oriented to ego-consciousness, opening up to them the realm of the transcendent. Also, for those in situations of evil, in which persons are totally possessed by personal or collective unconscious, Johannine symbolism can assure them that the light of consciousness can be brought to bear. Furthermore, those who are in analogical situations to that of the Johannine community, that is, personal or social alienation from the collective, will draw sustenance from the Gospel's symbols.

But there are limitations, and I would like to mention some cautions. Jung argued that Christ was not an appropriate symbol of the Self for the modern age because of the lack of darkness in him.[72] Indeed, this criticism weighs heaviest against the Fourth Gospel because alone in this Gospel does he say, "I am the light of the world. Whoever follows me will never walk in darkness but will have the light of life" (John 8:12). We must have the light of life in order that we might not be swallowed up in the darkness of unconscious. But if we identify so completely with the light, we lose touch with our own darkness and project it onto others, particularly those of a different race, gender, religion, socio-economic class, or political party.

We see the literary remains of such a psychological process in the Fourth Gospel itself. The Johannine community identified with Jesus as the light and projected their darkness onto the Jews. And, quite frankly, the church has been the worse ever since, for the Gospel has fueled anti-semitism. It is important to remember, though, that the picture of the Jews in the Fourth Gospel is a counter-projection. The Johannine community projected its shadow onto the synagogue authorities because that is what the synagogue authorities had done to the community. Perhaps the figure of the Jews in the Fourth Gospel can help the modern reader become conscious of—and withdraw—his or her own projections that are made onto others. Through reading about the shadow figure of the Jews in the Gospel, the reader can become conscious of the darkness within oneself.

We also need to evaluate the transformative possibilities of the symbols which are identified with Jesus, the symbol of the Self in the Gospel. The symbol of the shepherd comes to mind. Segovia criticized the use of this particular image because it has been used oppressively in missionary situations. The first-world missionary becomes the shepherd, and the third-world believers are the sheep, thus legitimating the authority of the missionary over the nationals.[73] David Miller has made a similar critique. He has argued that the image of the shepherd is perfectionistic and that it renders the believer in an infantile position.[74] He went on to supplement the image of Christ as the good shepherd with images from mythology such as ram and cyclops.[75]

Perhaps this is the way in which we need to move. The Johannine Jesus can only be a symbol of the Self if he is amplified with other images which can include darkness as well as light, evil as well as goodness. In doing so I think that we are in the spirit of the Fourth Gospel, in which Jesus says that God will send a Paraclete, the Spirit of truth, that will lead us into all truth (14:16; 16:13). This Spirit is with us and in us, emerging from the unconscious to bring us to wholeness.

A symbolic reading of the Fourth Gospel from the Jungian perspective therefore would see the Johannine symbols as symbols of transcendence, which reconcile unconscious and conscious, the world above and the world below. The Johannine symbolic world includes Jesus as the symbol of the Self—which is elaborated with various other symbols—female and male characters serving as anima and animus figures, and the Jews as the shadow figures. In the context of the Johannine community, these symbols functioned as compensation for the trauma of expulsion from the synagogue, so that the symbols of Judaism were reappropriated in terms of the new symbol of the Self, Jesus. Johannine symbols can still be transformative in the modern world, but limitations exist. Therefore, Jungian psychology gives a needed perspective on Johannine symbolism.

The Fourth Gospel ends with the following words: "But there are also many other things that Jesus did; if every one of them were written down, I suppose that the world itself could not contain the books that would be written" (21:25). The Gospel begins with the Word and ends with the inadequacy of words. So, in the end the reader is left with no more words, only experience—of God, of Christ, of truth, of glory, but also of Satan, of Antichrist, of falsehood, of suffering. One might say, then, that along with light, let there be darkness.[76]

❀ 4 ❀

The Myth Of Sophia

SCHUYLER BROWN

A ll the published writings of C. G. Jung pre-date the publication of the Coptic library of Gnostic texts found in 1945 in Upper Egypt near Nag Hammadi.[1] Jung's most in-depth consideration of Gnosis,[2] in *Aion*,[3] was first published in 1950; the first publication of a Nag Hammadi text, *The Gospel of Thomas*,[4] did not take place until 1959, just two years before Jung's death.[5]

Jung's knowledge of Gnosis and of the Sophia myth was, therefore, based on very limited source material.[6] Despite this fact, I find his understanding of the subject far more interesting and insightful than the work of some later scholars who have had many more sources at their disposal.

The reason for this is obvious. Academic students of Gnosis have adopted the "history of traditions" approach, which predominates in Biblical studies.[7] They have therefore studied the Gnostic writings with a view to reconstructing their ideas or doctrines. Jung, by contrast, recognized that the Gnostics, to an extent unparalleled in the canonical writings, allowed themselves to be influenced by inner experience. They are, therefore, "a veritable mine of information concerning all those natural symbols arising out of the repercussions of the Christian message."[8]

I shall begin this essay with one modern incarnation of Sophia and conclude with another. Jung believed that "there are archaic psychic components which have entered the individual psyche without any direct line of tradition."[9] The need for demonstrating literary dependence, which would be required in a "history of traditions" approach, is therefore superfluous.

I begin with the main character of Alban Berg's opera:

> Lulu, the irresistible is instinct. She has no father, no mother, no real name; she is called Nellie, Mignon, Eve and Lulu, and she doesn't know which is correct. She is at the same time pure, unspoiled nature and the ultimate in degeneracy—a murderess with no remorse, no morals, no feeling for right and wrong, pulsing with venom, lacking rational comprehension of her own lethal power. She is a naive, innocent, comely child, centuries old and newborn, with no past and no future. She is totally free and completely enslaved, victim and victimizer, always the same and always different. She lives for love, but she has no sense of love. She is beauty; she says she wants to be like nothing else in the world, so she is the epitome of beauty in all its forms—transient, everlasting, delightful, saddening, destructive, redeeming. There is nothing that can be done to her or about her. She is inevitable. It is not the flame's fault that the moth flies into it and is annihilated.[10]

Jung appears to be referring to a character very much like Lulu when he writes:

> The anima no longer crosses our path as a goddess, but, it may be, as an intimately personal misadventure, or perhaps our best venture. When, for instance, a highly esteemed professor in his seventies abandons his family and runs off with a young red-headed actress, we know that the gods have claimed another victim.[11]

The anima, of course, pertains to male psychology, and, as June Singer[12] and Joan Engelsman,[13] among others, have pointed out, Jung's teaching on the anima and the animus is in drastic need of revision. But Sophia is not limited to male psychology. Through her alter ego, Barbelo, she is part of the Godhead, and not simply an emanation or eon. She therefore functions for female psychology as a symbol of the Self. Jung's description of her continues:

> Although she may be the chaotic urge to life, something strangely meaningful clings to her, a secret knowledge or hidden wisdom, which contrasts most curiously with her irrational elfin nature. . . . Rider Haggard calls She "Wisdom's Daughter"; . . . Helen of Troy, in her incarnation, is rescued from a Tyrian brothel by the wise Simon Magus and accompanies him on his travels.[14]

Jung's reference to Simon and Helen alludes to a version of the Sophia myth based on the Acts of the Apostles, where Simon is referred to as "that power of God which is called great" (8:10).[15]

The union of opposites, which is so evident in these female figures, points to their archetypal nature:

> The first encounter with her [the anima] usually leads one to infer anything rather than wisdom. This aspect appears only to the person who gets to grips with her seriously. Only then, when this hard task has been faced, does he come to realize more and more that behind all her cruel sporting with human fate there lies something like a hidden purpose which seems to reflect a superior knowledge of life's laws. It is just the most unexpected, the most terrifyingly chaotic things which reveal a deeper meaning. And the more this meaning is recognized, the more the anima loses her impetuous and compulsive character. Gradually breakwaters are built against the surging of chaos, and the meaningful divides itself from the meaningless.[16]

The oldest versions of the Sophia myth are found in the Hebrew Bible and the Greek Old Testament, those sections of scripture which are called "Wisdom Literature." One of the most famous of these texts, Prov. 8: 22–31, begins with a verse which could be translated: "The Lord acquired me as an archetype of his work."[17] Sophia is not God's creature; she is as eternal as God himself. She is the plan according to which creation proceeds and to which God himself is bound. She is the connecting principle between the deity and creation. On the one hand, she is God's "delight" (v. 30)—a reflection of the androgynous deity which we encounter in the Gnostic texts, and, on the other, she "delights" (v. 31) to be among the children of men.

M.-L. von Franz refers to Sophia as "an awkward figure for Christian theologians,"[18] and this awkwardness finds expression in the following assessment:

> In these poetic passages many have seen a description of a divine person, distinct from God and operating independently of Him. Such an idea is quite wrong. . . . A convinced monotheist, as the author of the Book of Wisdom certainly is, would never think of regarding divine wisdom as really a bride, seated beside Him on a throne, for that would make a genuine goddess out of wisdom. If this detail in his description of wisdom must be regarded as purely metaphorical, so also must all the rest of the description.

> Most modern exegetes admit that divine wisdom in the Old
> Testament is no divine person.[19]

Not only is Sophia deprived of her divine status; she is also split
off from her sister, Folly, who, in the following chapter of Proverbs, lies in wait for the unwary, calling out: "Stolen water is
sweet, and bread eaten in secret is pleasant" (9:17). For Jung,
"wisdom and folly appear as one and the same,"[20] but in the
Wisdom Literature of the Old Testament the archetype is split,
and the opposites are no longer united.

Jung's principal argument with orthodox Christianity was
over its refusal to acknowledge the shadow in the deity and the
consequent demonizing of the shadow in our own psyche.
Martin Buber attacked Jung's concept of the Self as made up of
a unity of opposites, including good and evil. He considered this
concept to be a form of moral libertinism. But for Jung shadow
assimilation in consciousness entails the painful and steadfast
acknowledgment of the potential for evil in one's own being. This
is the first step in its transformation and appropriation in an
expanded and safer consciousness. "Understood within the context of Jung's psychology, such rigorous honesty is a far cry
from moral irresponsibility."[21]

Following an intense confrontation with shadow projection, a
woman wrote the following poem:

> Don't forget the Shadow
> of your nights,
> those darkly etched shades
> that lie so passively
> waiting
> to seep under the door
> of sleep
> and, like smoke,
> surround you with another
> reflection of yourself.
>
> Open wide the door of night
> locked against this fearful Other.
> Welcome the Shadow
> as friend.
> She is no stranger.
> She is no enemy.
> The face she wears
> is your own,

and, like you,
she too is afraid.
Left so long in darkness,
feeding on her rage and sorrow
she grows strong and powerful.
But unclaimed power can destroy as
unloved strength loses control
and these forces
can corrupt beauty
and betray creation.

Redemption of the soul
comes from suffering
this darkling force
as it struggles
to save you from a life
of collective attitudes
and collective responses.
Liberation from unconscious Being
and repeated behaviors
that lead to nowhere,
demands this joining
of light and dark.

Trembling
with pounding heart
and clenched stomach
I beg you
open the door of night
and let the Shadow in.

Face her—humbly, bravely
and with love—
for it is she alone
who can guide you
from the night shades
to the morning sun.

E. A.[22]

By contrast, the canonical Book of Wisdom insists on the one-sided purity of the feminine archetype:

> She is a breath of the power of God, and a pure emanation of the glory of the Almighty; therefore nothing defiled gains entrance into her. For she is a reflection of eternal light, a spotless mirror of the working of God, and an image of his goodness (7:26–27).

Truth to tell, the archetypal feminine does not readily fit into either Jewish or Christian monotheism. In modern biblical scholarship, Wisdom is regarded *merely* as a personification, and this personification is *merely* poetic license. Here, clearly, we see the conflict between historical, doctrinal, and mythological ways of thinking.

The world of Gnosis, now extensively illustrated through the Nag Hammadi texts, is a world from which mythological thinking has not yet been banished in the interest of doctrinal and ethical uniformity. The fascination of Gnosis is that it reveals what Christianity might have been, and what Christianity might yet become. Gnosis treats the Christian symbols as expressions of the creative imagination, rather than as metaphysical realities.[23] Such mythological understanding returns the Christian symbols to the psychic matrix from which they have come and removes the barrier between religion and experience which Jung found to be the greatest weakness of Western religion.

Gnosis builds a bridge not only between Christianity and the psyche but also between Christianity and other religions, especially the great religious traditions of the East, which have never adopted the extraverted religious attitude of Western Christianity.

To recognize the proximity of the Nag Hammadi texts to experience is not to suggest that their authors were successfully individuated human beings.[24] But, beyond all question, these writers were open to the unconscious in a way which becomes increasingly rare in Christianity, outside the mystical tradition.

Gnosis used to be dismissed, along with alchemy, as a degenerate product of late antiquity. There is much that can be adduced to support this verdict, specifically, the Gnostics' negative attitude towards the body, sexuality, and the whole of material creation. To go into this matter in depth would take us too far afield. It is sufficient to point out that such negative attitudes were widespread in late antiquity; they were not a specifically Gnostic phenomenon.

Moreover, although the Gnostics consciously repudiated sexuality, it becomes the root metaphor in their literature for both creation and redemption. This, in fact, is what most clearly distinguishes Gnosis from Jewish and Christian orthodoxy, where the word, rather than the sexual act, is the means of creation. To use Freudian terminology, the imaginative language of the Gnostics prefers primary to secondary process.

This metaphoric use of sexuality in Gnostic texts recalls Jung's dispute with Freud over libido, which Jung refused to limit to the sexual instinct but extended to psychic energy in whatever form.[25]

Sexuality is the root metaphor behind the Sophia myth, in which the creation of the world is attributed to Sophia's desire "to reveal the likeness [of her thought] out of herself, although the spirit had not consented or granted [it], nor again had her partner consented, the male virgin spirit."[26] Sexuality is also operative in the Gnostic interpretation of the Adam and Eve story: "When Eve was still in Adam, death did not exist. When she separated from him, death came into being. If he enters again and attains his former self, death will be no more."[27]

The reintegration of masculine and feminine, symbolized by the sexual act ("he enters"), takes place in the sacrament of the bridal chamber, through which the soul (conceived of as feminine) is reunited with her angelic counterpart (conceived of as masculine). This sacrament is "the holy of the holies,"[28] and it ranks above the other sacraments. Its object is to anticipate the final union, which takes place at death.[29]

The Gnostics treasured those incidents in the gospels which described the close relationship of Christ with women in his circle, especially Mary Magdalene. Through the chaste kiss of fellowship the firmest links in the human chain are formed, for "it is by a kiss that the perfect conceive and give birth."[30] In the transmission of esoteric teaching, the Gnostics possessed "the ethereal secret of perpetual self-reproduction."[31]

Scholars of Gnosis often interpret the ideal of androgyny as though it were the replacement of sexuality through an asexual neuter. Those who read these texts from a Jungian perspective see androgyny rather as a symbolic representation of psychic complementarity, including both the masculine and feminine aspects which are present in every individual personality, regardless of biological gender.

This difference in interpretation points to a basic problem with much scholarship on Gnosis: the lack of appreciation for the symbolic dimension, which leads to literalism in interpretation. The Gnostics despised the body as a symbol of ignorance and forgetfulness. The coming of the soul into matter makes it forget its heavenly origin and become involved in worldly cares.

The role of Gnosis is to provide a wake-up call which reminds the soul of its origin and destiny, so that it awakes from the nightmare of worldly existence.[32] Freud's famous saying, "Stop repeating and start remembering," illustrates the psychological significance of the Gnostics' concern with forgetfulness.

In blaming the body for the soul's forgetfulness and in making it the scapegoat for human ignorance, the Gnostics were simply projecting onto the body *their own* ignorance of the body itself. Most of us are still profoundly ignorant of our own bodies, for the body is "the Other" *par excellence*. It is not the cause of our ignorance; rather, it is that of which *we* are still unconscious. Bringing light into matter is the Gnostic task. Even if we are to be liberated from the world, as the Gnostics believed, the world and the body remain the place where this liberation must occur.

The darkly pessimistic Gnostic world view should not lead us to dismiss an approach to Christian symbolism which has profound psychological significance, and the potential to renew the faltering structures of Western religion. Gnosis is one of the great moments of the power of myth in the ancient world. That power has been absent in Christianity since Gnosis was repressed, and it is sorely needed today.

The story of Sophia's attempt to conceive without a consort, the abortion which resulted, and her repentance and restoration to the heavenly world, all this is unfolded with incredible complexity in a number of writings from the Nag Hammadi corpus. It is not possible even to summarize them here.[33]

However, from a Jungian perspective, it is easy to see the psychological correspondences with the main protagonists in the drama. The pleroma, or heavenly world, corresponds to the unconscious; the ignorant demiurge, or creator god, to the human ego, which vainly boasts: "I am a jealous God; apart from me there is no other" (Exod. 20:5; Isa. 45:5). The archons, who are the creation of the demiurge, yet hostile towards him, suggest the complexes, which are never entirely under the ego's control. Sophia herself, as we have already suggested, functions both as the anima and as the Self.

But such an allegorization of the Sophia myth would fall back into the doctrinal mode of interpretation to which I referred earlier. The proximity of these texts to the unconscious stirs up unconscious contents in us, breaking our grip on the fixed structures of objectivity and referentiality, and drawing us into the vortex of inner process. This literature should not be read for too long at one sitting!

In Gnosis the archetype which was fractured in the canonical scripture is restored as a union of opposites. In *The Thunder, Perfect Mind,* a female figure delivers a revelatory discourse which expresses Sophia's two manners of existence: perfect, divine, redeeming power, and fallen woman:

> I am the honoured and the despised
> I am the prostitute and the respectable woman
> I am the wife and the virgin
> I am the mother and the daughter
> I am the members of my mother.[34]

> I am the silence which is unattainable
> The insight which much in the world recalls
> I am the voice whose sound is manifold
> And the logos which has many images.[35]

> I am knowledge and ignorance
> I am shame and boldness
> I am shameless and I am ashamed
> I am strength and I am fear.[36]

A simpler form of the complex creation myth is found in a beautiful work entitled *The Exegesis on the Soul,* Beverly Moon, a student of Elaine Pagels, has written the following summary:

> In the beginning, that is, before the Fall, the soul was actually an androgynous being that existed in the proximity of God the Father. At the same time, there existed, separately, the lower world, over which ruled the goddess Aphrodite, the divine principle of generation. The feminine half of the androgynous soul is attracted to Aphrodite's realm of becoming, and so she falls into corporeal existence. The fallen soul is called Psyche. She is represented as a woman who, while seeking for her lost mate, attaches herself helter-skelter to the so-called robbers of creation: the impermanent affairs of the phenomenal order.

> In the world of constant flux, each attachment must inevitably come to an end. Furthermore, each union of Psyche and the robbers yields only imperfect fruit: their children are lame and mentally deficient. Eventually, in despair that all her efforts must lead ultimately nowhere, Psyche gives up. She weeps and calls out for help. So now the Father hears her and decides to send down her masculine counterpart, the spirit-giving brother, who is identified as the Christ, to rescue her.

But first, God the Father prepares Psyche for this event by baptiz-
ing her. He restores her womb, which during the Fall had become
externalized, like the male genitalia. The restoration of Psyche's
womb within gives her once again the capacity for an inner, or
spiritual, receptivity (as opposed to the compulsion to find fulfillment in external attachments). Psyche, for her part, beautifies the
Bridal Chamber, where she then receives her spirit-giving bride-
groom. Their union results in the rebirth of the original androg-
yne, which is able to ascend at once to the Father.[37]

In conclusion, I present a second modern incarnation of Sophia,
but this time, in contrast to Lulu's lethal destructiveness, Sophia
has a smiling face. The character is the heroine of the film, "Pretty
Woman," and I am citing from a brilliant study by Priscilla Costello.

The excerpt is from the final scene of the film, which Ms.
Costello thinks may be the most significant. The two characters
are Edward, a wealthy New York businessman, and Vivian, a
hooker with a heart of gold:

> At the end of the film the symbolism of Edward coming from the
> upper world into the fallen world to rescue Vivian/Sophia is
> reversed. It is she who is "above," in a top-floor apartment, and
> Edward has once again to overcome his fears by climbing up to
> be with her. "It had to be the top floor, right?" he comments.
> "It's the best," she counters. "All right, I'm coming up," he says.
> Thus, Sophia, who was earlier below, in her fallen state, is now
> above. The final dialogue refers to a conversation which the two
> had had at the hotel just before Vivian left: she told him of her
> childhood fantasy of pretending she was a princess locked in a
> tower who would be rescued by a prince. Edward's climb up her
> fire escape is the equivalent of the ascent of the fairy-tale tower.
> Vivian comes down one level to meet Edward, and he asks her,
> "So what happened after the prince climbed up the tower and
> rescued her?" She answers, "She rescues him right back."[38]

The two faces of Sophia are a reflection of her nature as a life
force. Life includes both good and evil, and whoever wants life
wills both the bitter and the sweet. But the face of Sophia which
comes into view depends upon the stance which the individual
takes to the archetype herself. For the individual who resists life
by refusing to enter upon the path of individuation, Sophia takes
on a seductive or even destructive appearance. But for the individual who gives Sophia the respect which she deserves, she
becomes a spiritual guide, a psychopomp, and a bridge to the creative energy of the unconscious.

❦ AFTERWORD ❦

Biblical Imagery And Psychological Likeness

DAVID L. MILLER

The essays of this book represent a remarkable hermeneutical experiment. For one hundred years the theorists and practitioners of depth psychology, especially the followers of Freud and Jung, have attended to and have interpreted biblical texts for which they had no particular and direct expertise. On the other side, there have been, since the Second World War, but not often, a few biblical scholars who have drawn upon psychological resources for purposes of interpretation of sacred text. Notable instances come immediately to mind: Dan Via, Phyllis Tribble, Mary Ann Tolbert, Richard Rubenstein, Walter Wink, William Wuellner, Robin Scroggs, and Gerd Theissen. But until Wayne Rollins convened a psychological section in the Society for Biblical Literature and until Trevor Watt hosted a conference on the psychological interpretation of the Bible at Canissius College in Buffalo, New York, there has been nothing that could have been conceived of as a concerted movement in which persons trained formally in biblical criticism petitioned depth psychological insights for hermeneutical purposes.

The reader will have noted from the preceding chapters that the movement, as represented in this book, is not monolithic, perhaps not even a "movement." Even when it is the psychology of C. G. Jung that is appropriated interpretively, as is the case with the present authors, there is no question of psychological orthodoxy of canon or interpretation. On the other hand, there is also no question of what Jung once referred to as "banality."

Jung had been asked in 1958 what would happen if Jesus were to return to the earth. He responded that, because of the media attention, "he would see himself banalized beyond all endurance."[1] Jung's choice of words was apt (he wrote this in English to a magazine editor in the United States). Originally the term "banal" referred to a kind of feudal service whereby the tenants of a certain district were obliged to carry their grain to be ground at a certain mill and to be baked at a certain oven to the economic benefit of the lord of the manor. Though the word denotes "commonness," it implies, not variety and difference, but monopoly.

One might have conceived former tendencies in biblical interpretation to have been banal in both senses—i.e., having become in our time a bit common historiographically and theologically. But this is as a result of monopolistic perspective, even though, at first blush, it would appear that there has actually existed a hermeneutic binarism since the eighteenth century.

On the one hand, there seems to have been an assumption by some that the text of the Bible has doctrinal referents. That is, it is taken for granted in this perspective that biblical representation ultimately signifies tenets of belief, that the images and narratives of various pericopes have to do with ideas and thoughts to which a person in our own day may either give assent in faith or not. This places the signifying function of the biblical text in the realm of what philosophers call intelligibles.

But on the other hand, different interpreters (or the same interpreters at different times or with different texts) seem to have assumed that the referent of the biblical text had to do with sensible rather than intelligible reality. It refers, these persons imagine, historically, and its message points to doings and experiences rather than being and meaning.

As biblical scholarship has swung back and forth between these (largely unconscious) hermeneutic perspectives, the effect on the religious imagination has been to split dogma and piety, mind and heart, spirit and flesh, ideal and real, thought and feeling, infinite and finite, supernature and nature, transcendental

and immanent. Yet these binarisms do not indicate real difference. Rather, philosophically understood, they both are represen-
tational and referential with regard to signification and thereby
carry an unwitting metaphysics of presence as a part of their per-
spectival baggage. Psychologically put, they locate religion psychologically as a function of ego (ego's beliefs and doctrines and
thoughts and ideas, or ego's experiences and history and behaviors). Further, this monopolistic binarism (an ontotheology of ego)
tends to locate the function of a religious text in the past (history,
Heilsgeschichte, the sins of the Fathers) or in the future (the
Kingdom, eschatology, tomorrow's moral imperative). What is
missed is the psychological possibility that there is an impact of
biblical imagery in the here-and-now, a signifying that is different
from without being opposed to historical or theological meanings,
a textual intentionality and function that refers to a dimension of
selfhood that is other than ego.

To put the matter another way, if assuming a theological and
doctrinal significance to texts puts the interpreter in a deductive
and rationalistic mode of thinking, and if assuming a historical
and experiential significance implies an inductive and empirical
strategy, there is yet a third possible way. The historian of religions, Henry Corbin, called this alternative by the name *mundus
imaginalis*, which was his translation into Latin of the Arabic
alam-al-mithal.[2] This "imaginal realm" functions similarly to the
celebrated *metaxy* of Plato and of Plotinus, for both of whom the
"middle realm," between mind's intelligibles (*nous*) and experience's sensibles (*aisthetikoi*), is the domain of soul (*psychē*) and
carries the workings of imagination (*phantasia*).

This "between realm" can be understood from everyday experience. If I attempt to communicate an idea to someone who
does not understand, I might offer an illustration (i.e., giving
image to an otherwise abstract deduction). On the other hand, if
I try to communicate an experience to someone who has never
had such an experience, I might give a likeness or metaphor
(i.e., giving image to an otherwise idiosyncratic empirical reality).
Not only can the person sense the likeness of the idea or experience in the image, but she or he also and simultaneously is able
to have a feel for the idea or a cognition concerning the experience. Idea and experience come together in imagination's

images. From Corbin's perspective, imagery functions in a modality other than that of reason and sensation. Yet, it integrates these epistemic aspects that otherwise tend to split off from each other.

Think of the Bible in this imaginal manner.[3] The biblical text is a treasure-house of images that are contextualized in a variety of genres (myth, history, parable, poetry, letter, prophecy, and apocalypse). These may be viewed not only as historical and/or eschatological, but also as profound psychological life-likenesses. For example, we are thrown into a world where things need naming; excluded from paradisical bliss; confused by the world's towering Babel; deluged and flooded; in bondage; yet from time to time we are able to walk dry through the seas' tempests and over the waves, even if it leads to more wilderness wandering; we are drawn to idols of gold and want a king like the others; are exiled on an ash heap, yet experience guidance from our whirlwinds; even discover that something sacred is born from a virginal place; we also have been nailed, betrayed by our nearest friend, torn to pieces; and yet, miraculously, we manage to go on after three days or so; find ourselves waiting for spirit to come; and experience apocalypse now: "My God, my God! Why hast Thou forsaken me?" This is as articulate a psychology as one can find anywhere. The biblical images are as-structures of the ideas (fantasies) and feelings of the psyche.

Freud and Jung, who were otherwise drawn to Greek mythological images for their psychological tropings, both knew this psychological dimension of the Bible, as well as the biblical dimension of the modern psyche. It is not surprising to find Jung saying that "we must read the Bible or we shall not understand psychology. Our psychology, whole lives, our language and images are built upon the Bible."[4] But Freud's concurring words may for some be unanticipated: "My deep engrossment in the Bible story (almost as soon as I had learnt the art of reading) had, as I recognized much later, an enduring effect on the direction of my interest."[5]

If the psychological hermeneutical discovery is more obvious after Freud and Jung, it is nonetheless not new. The here-and-now life-likeness approach to biblical texts was, to give only one example, already defended by Origen of Alexandria. In his work,

On First Principals, Origen was worrying the problem of a discrepancy between the twenty-sixth and the twenty-seventh verses of the first chapter of Genesis. He wrote: "'And God said, Let us make man in our own image and likeness.' Then he [Moses] adds afterward, 'And God made man; in the image of God made he him. . . .' Now the fact that he said, He made him in the image of God, and was silent about the likeness, points to nothing else but this, that man received the honor of God's image in the first creation, whereas the perfection of God's likeness was reserved for him."[6] The implication for biblical study is that the text of the Bible reveals a world of images that are given by God, but that the work of men and women in this life is to continue the creation of worlds of meaning by seeing likenesses among these images and with life, as in the examples given two paragraphs above.

To be sure, not everyone is convinced. Typical critiques of a psychological hermeneutic of the Bible, and especially of an archetypal Jungian interpretive strategy, fall into three categories: essentialism, comparativism, and reductionism. I should like to address each of these reticences in turn.

ESSENTIALISM/DIFFERENCE

One typical criticism of a Jungian or archetypal textual interpretation goes somewhat as follows: by assuming that the imagery has archetypal psychological intentionality one implies a world of essences and essential forms of human meaning. The problem with such an assumption—or so goes the critique—is that it does not have adequate regard for the otherness of the divine or for the otherness of other persons. It elides, not only the "infinite qualitative distinction" between the divine and human, but also the fundamental differences of persons of various races, classes, and genders.

This criticism is, however, unsophisticated about the notion of "archetype." Ironically, it is a criticism concerning difference that fails to draw upon an important difference, a difference that is poignantly illustrated by an anecdote about C. G. Jung and Mircea Eliade.

In the context of their friendship at Eranos Conferences, Eliade, late in 1954, sent Jung a copy of his then new book on yoga. The former speaks in that work about what he takes to be the archetypal significance of mandala images from South Asian yogic contexts and he quotes Jung in support of his point about these being structurally archetypal. Eliade clearly thought that he was agreeing with what he took to be Jung's universal and essentialist point on the appearance of similar imagery in his patients' spontaneous drawings. But much to Eliade's astonishment, instead of receiving a pleasant thank you note, Jung sent in reply a diatribe that indicated a profound difference between a philosophical (Platonic-Augustinian) use of the notion of archetype as an essential intellectual form, i.e., Eliade's notion, and a depth psychological use of what many wrongly assume is the same notion.[7] So crucial was the difference to Jung that it seems nearly to have destroyed the personal friendship between the two men. However, Eliade changed the citation to Jung in a later edition of the work and wrote an apologetic clarification in the introduction of a still later book.[8]

The difference in the two ideas concerning archetype may be understood as the difference between material likenesses of something that does appear among images that seem to be the same as opposed to formal likenesses of something that does not appear (unconscious) among images that differ. Plotinus calls this distinction the difference between likenesses of like things (which the philosopher takes to be superficial) as opposed to the likenesses of unlike things (that is, a likeness that does not appear and that is based upon difference).[9] The former tends to stereotype. Jung wants to reserve the idea of archetype for the latter (even if many Jungians in our time themselves seem to entertain the same confusion as did Eliade).

Jung was firmly post-Kantian concerning essence and difference, even if his language side-slipped from time to time. He saw clearly that the so-called "self" is the object and the subject of the psychological work and that all psychological knowledge was therefore hypothetical, having no claim to universal essentialist validity, and was thereby confessional by nature.[10] This implies that "archetype" is by no means a metaphysical postulate, but is heuristic in function.[11] Jung's own strategy in psychological interpretation was to focus upon difference. Individuation (advance in psychological insight) was thought of as differentiation rather than as identification, the separation of the parts of a whole rather than an achievement of wholeness (the latter of which Jung thought impossible).[12] Individuation is, he said, a becoming of that which one is not, and it is accompanied by the feeling of being a stranger.[13] So much is this the case that it has led James Hillman, a postmodern archetypalist after Jung, not to use the word "archetype" as a noun (as if it referred to some "things" or essences), but rather to use the word "archetypal," which Hillman says "is a move one makes rather than a thing that is."[14]

It is the archetypal "move" that is being made by the essays in the preceding chapters, and it is a "move" that is hardly vulnerable to an essentialist critique. This criticism is a misunderstanding, indeed, a projection. It could be argued that an authentically Jungian hermeneutic precisely de-essentializes the meaning of the text, rather than locating what someone might think of as an essential meaning or a psychological essence. Biblical images as life-likenesses are liknesses based on fundamental difference rather than sameness. They are (un)grounded upon that which the person is not, upon otherness with which the psyche, though different from, resonates.

Comparativism/Historicism

A second critique of a Jungian hermeneutic fears any archetypal reading of meaning in the name of particularistic difference: namely, historical and temporal distinctiveness. The criticism is that an archetypal interpretation wittingly or unwittingly presupposes that meaning in texts is separate and separable from its social, historical, and political context. The images of a narrative or a poem—so goes this assumption (or so it is assumed)—signify similarly across temporal and spatial boundaries. A Jungian archetypalism leads inevitably to a comparativism in which everything is finally everything. It is likeness run amuck, devoid of real reality.

A first response to this charge must entail a reality-check in the form of a few statements by Jung himself on the issue that is at stake. In order to make the point as strongly as possible, and to avoid in advance the counter-charge of selecting an isolated text out of context, I shall cite four of Jung's remarks:

Primordial images and the nature of the archetype took a central place in my researches, and it became clear to me that without history there can be no psychology, and certainly no psychology of the unconscious. A psychology of consciousness can, to be sure, content itself with material taken from personal life, but as soon as we wish to explain a neurosis we require an anamnesis which reaches deeper than the knowledge of consciousness.[15]

It is . . . a grave mistake to think that it is enough to gain some understanding of the images and that knowledge here can make a halt. Insight into them must be converted into an ethical obligation. Not to do so is to fall prey to the power principle and this produces dangerous effects which are destructive not only to others but even to the knower.[16]

For me . . . irreality was the quintessence of horror, for I aimed, after all, at this world and this life. No matter how deeply absorbed or how blown about I was, I always knew that everything I was experiencing was ultimately directed at this real life of mine.[17]

[Speaking of Christianity] Everything has its history, everything has "grown," and Christianity, which is supposed to have appeared suddenly as a sudden revelation from heaven, undoubtedly also has its history. . . . It is exactly as if we had built a cathedral over a pagan temple and no longer know that it is there unendingly.[18]

These citations have at least the complicating effect of putting in the mouth of Jung the very words some critics use against him, which suggests that the supposed critique may well be itself a psychological projection that is intentionally or unintentionally ill informed and lacking in serious scholarship. There is, therefore, a certain irony in critics of Jung's purported ahistoricism being themselves not altogether realistically contextualized. But the matter is as complex as it is ironic.

Jonathan Z. Smith has quoted Burton Mack approvingly concerning the matter that Jung refers to above concerning the ahistorical nature of certain historicist hermeneutics of Christianity:

The fundamental persuasion [of many scholars] is that Christianity appeared unexpectedly in human history, that it was (is) at core a brand new vision of human existence, and that, since this is so, only a startling moment could account for its emergence at the beginning. The code word serving as a sign for

the novelty that appeared is the term unique. . . . It is this startling moment that seems to have mesmerized the discipline and
determined the application of its critical methods.[19]

The point, I take it, is that the so-called historical hermeneutic of Christianity since the Enlightenment has given a reading
of Christianity that is ahistorical, that denies Christianity's historical context. This suggests that the historical critique of
archetypal hermeneutics as ahistorical has itself been involved
in a reading of Christianity that is archetypal and ahistorical,
whereas Jung wants archetypal readings to be grounded historically and to have political and real-life effects.

The larger problem with this comparativist-historicist binarism is that it may well have been a false split from the beginning. Jonathan Z. Smith has already been mentioned, and it has
been his work for the past twenty years or so to correct a sim-
plistic dualism concerning this matter. Smith is presurring the
unwitting assumption that Nietzsche's Zarathustra calls "the
myth of the immaculate perception," that is, the naively realistic
assumption that historical readings bear a transparency to some
past real reality free of interpretative perspective.

Smith's point has been that differentiating historical work
always and already involves comparison. In a lecture at Arizona
State University in 1985, Smith gave examples of St. Paul, John
of Plan del Carpini, and Jan von Ruysbroeck, as well as the
Israelites in the Bible, to show that "a theory of difference, when
applied to the proximate 'other,' is but another way of para-
phrasing a theory of 'self.'"[20] Smith called this "differential equations," and he noted that if there were "actual remoteness,"
authentic historical otherness and some fundamental and separable difference, there would be "mutual indifference." It is not a
matter of whether comparativist identifications take place in his-
toriography, it is rather only a matter of whether they are made
conscious or not. Jungian hermeneutics becomes a convenient
scapegoat for historians who may be unconsciously anxious
about the subjective nature of their objective work. Think about
the histories written about the Civil War.

Furthermore, as Smith says in an earlier work, "comparison
itself requires the postulation of difference as the grounds of its
being interesting (rather than tautological) and a methodological

manipulation of difference, a playing across the 'gap' in the service of some useful end."[21] Just as historical particularism implies comparison, so comparison implies difference and particularity. So, Smith says: "The process of comparison is a fundamental characteristic of human intelligence. Whether revealed in the logical grouping of classes, in poetic similes, in mimesis, or other like activities—comparison, the bringing together of two or more objects for the purpose of noting either similarity or dissimilarity, is the omni-present substructure of human thought."[22] This is, of course, the point about seeing life-likenesses of biblical images and, to be sure, it is a very historical and particular activity, as the preceding essays in this book have shown.

In his recent book, *The Savage in Judaism,* Howard Eilberg-Schwartz has made an argument that is adjacent to Smith's and that reveals the naiveté of the historicist critique of an archetypal comparativism. Eilberg-Schwartz writes: "Determining what is 'the context' is itself always an interpretive act. . . ."[23] That is, the distinction between a historical contextualist and a comparativist paradigm breaks down in the end. Is Jewish religion and history the context for Christian origins? Should the social and historical context be extended to Greco-Roman culture? Egyptian? And if these, should one not note the Persian and Indian contextualizations? And East Asian? Eilberg-Schwartz notes what must be apparent, but is often not acknowledged: "Comparative analysis is simply unavoidable. If an interpreter repudiates it, it comes in the back door."[24] "History, like ethnography, always already presupposes comparative inquiry. . . . What this means is that there is no escaping the comparative enterprise. Even the most concrete, contextualist study presupposes certain notions about societies, cultures, and persons formulated to explain human behavior and experience in diverse contexts."[25] To put this matter provocatively, one might say that everyone is Jungian! That is, every textual interpretation is *eo ipso* archetypal (in Jung's sense, but not in Eliade's). The biblical scholars in this book are owning this fact and attempting to take advantage of it in their work.

Psychologism/Reductionism

A third typical critique remains, even if these other two were able to be met satisfactorily. It is the familiar charge of humanization of things divine, of bringing the larger into the domain of the smaller, of the reductionism of psychologism.

Surely reductionism is a perduring risk. To be sure, one wonders if it is any more a risk in psychological than in historical and theological readings. Nonetheless, there are many humanistic psychological readings that reduce. Indeed, Jung complained in the Tavistock Lectures that Freud's method of "free association" was reductive and offered his own "seeking the parallels" in larger archetypal contexts (myth, folktale, religion, the arts) as a corrective in the direction of "amplification," seeing the smaller in terms of the larger, what Proclus calls *epistrophē*, a "leading back" of human things to their larger archetypal contexts.

Just here is the point. A given interpretation that proceeds by seeing life-likenesses in biblical images may indeed itself be interpreted as reductive. But it may also be imagined otherwise. Rather than being a matter of psychologizing the Bible, it can be understood as the experience of "biblicizing" the psyche, of imagining human thoughts and feelings in terms of biblical images, divinizing the human rather than humanizing the divine. It is not that Jacob and his mother and father are in an oedpial complex, but rather that a given sense of the familial mess can be seen as a Jacob complex.

This is a taking seriously of Jung's saying that "we must read the Bible or we shall not understand psychology." It is what Heinz Westman had in mind when he attempted with historical and psychological realism to acknowledge that his patients had biblical as well as greco-roman complexes, that the Bible is the "code," not only of Western literature (as Northrop Frye has noted), but also and equally tacitly that it is one of the codes of the Western psyche. (See Westman's books: *The Springs of Creativity* and *The Structure of Biblical Myths*.)

The hermeneutic goal is a psychology understood in biblical figures, not a biblical text understood egoically. Jung's heuristic is called "depth" psychology precisely because it is not reductive (not an ego-psychology), though one may be in fact reductive by not taking realistic account of the profound aspects of selfhood occasioned by biblical insight. As Walter Wink once said: "We have analyzed the Bible; now we may wish to find ways to let it analyze us."[26] That is what the experiment represented by this book is about.

❧ NOTES ❧

Introduction

1. Most of the material in this essay is excerpted or adapted from the manuscript of the author's book, *The Bible in Psychological Perspective*, to be published by Fortress Press.
2. C. G. Jung, *The Visions Seminars*, vol. 1 (Zürich: Spring Publications, 1976), 156. Cited by: Edward Edinger, *The Bible and the Psyche: Individuation Symbolism in the Old Testament* (Toronto: Inner City Books, 1986), 11.
3. C. G. Jung, *Letters*, vol. 1, ed. G. Adler and A. Jaffé, trans. R. F. C. Hull (Princeton: Princeton University Press, 1973), 463, addressed to Frau Schmit-Lohner, May 20, 1947.
4. C. G. Jung, *Letters*, vol. 2, ed. G. Adler and A. Jaffé, trans. R. F. C. Hull (Princeton: Princeton University Press, 1975), 85.
5. Robin Scroggs, "Psychology as a Tool to Interpret the Text," *Christian Century* (March 24, 1982): 335.
6. Gerd Theissen, *Psychological Aspects of Pauline Theology*, trans. J. P. Galvin. (Minneapolis: Fortress Press, 1987), 1.
7. Werner George Kümmel, *The New Testament: The History of the Investigation of its Problems*, trans. S. M. Gilmour and H. C. Kee (Nashville: Abingdon, 1972), 93–95, 149, 152, 237.
8. Albert Schweitzer, *The Psychiatric Study of Jesus: Exposition and Criticism* [1913], trans. C. R. Joy. (Boston: Beacon Press, 1948), 7, 74.
9. Vincent Taylor chronicles the fact that Sanday's "well known attempt to apply the findings of psychology to Christology" were "rejected on all sides." See: Vincent Taylor, *The Person of Christ in New Testament Teaching* (London: Macmillan, 1959), 278.
10. Noteworthily, Bultmann, in *Theology of the New Testament* vol. I, lists the works of Delitzsch, Fletcher, and H. Wheeler Robinson on "biblical psychology" apropos of his sections on "psyche" and anthropology, presumably affirming the legitimacy of reconstructing a biblical "psychology" without using the term, even though the history of its use is well established since the reformation as an aspect of biblical anthropology.
11. Cf. Theissen, *Psychological Aspects of Pauline Theology*, on Gunkel, 268, and on Bousset, 16. On Johannes Weiss, cf. Kümmel, *The New Testament*, 280.

12. "Current Issues in New Testament Study," *Harvard Divinity School Bulletin* 19 (1953): 54.

13. Robinson uses the term "psychology" in the classical post-Reformation sense as a branch of anthropology that seeks to identify the biblical understanding of the origin, nature, and destiny of the human "psyche." See: H. Wheeler Robinson, "The Psychology of Inspiration," *Inspiration and Revelation in the Old Testament* (Oxford: Clarendon, 1946), 173–187.

14. Walter Wink's hyperbolic statement in 1973, that "historical biblical criticism is bankrupt," chronicles the beginnings of the shift. See: Walter Wink, *The Bible in Human Transformation: Towards a New Paradigm for Biblical Study* (Philadelphia: Fortress Press, 1973).

15. John Dominic Crossan, "Perspectives and Methods in Contemporary Biblical Criticism," *Biblical Research* 22 (1977): 41.

16. The document of the Pontifical Biblical Commission may be found in: "The Interpretation of the Bible in the Church," *Catholic International* 3/5 (1994): 109–147 (the citations in the text are from 122–23 and 109).

17. Joachim Scharfenberg, *Sigmund Freud and His Critique of Religion*, trans. O. C. Dean, Jr. (Philadelphia: Fortress Press, 1988), 12.

18. H. L. Philp, *Freud and Religious Belief* (New York: Pitman Publishing Corporation, 1956), 94.

19. Scharfenberg, *Sigmund Freud and His Critique of Religion*, 27, who also notes that Freud's biographer, Ernest Jones, found this statement "incomprehensible."

20. Philp, *Freud and Religious Belief*, 92.

21. Jung, *Letters*, 2. 359.

22. Ibid., 346.

23. C. G. Jung, *Memories, Dreams, Reflections*, ed. Aniela Jaffé, trans. R. and C. Winston (New York: Pantheon, 1963), 43.

24. C. G. Jung, *CW*, 12.13 (see the bibliography entry at the end of the book for an explanation of the manner of notation of the *Collected Works* of Jung).

25. C. G. Jung, "Approaching the Unconscious," *Man and His Symbols* (New York: Doubleday and Co., 1971), 102.

26. Jung, "Approaching the Unconscious," 94.

27. Jung, *CW*, 11.52.

28. Jung, *Memories, Dreams, Reflections*, 55.

29. Jung, *CW*, 8.528.

30. Ibid., 11.748–51.

31. Jung, *Letters*, 2.206.

32. Jung, *CW*, 11.34.

33. Jung, *Letters*, 2.88, 89, 91.

34. Ibid., 115–16.

35. Jung, *Memories, Dreams, Reflections*, 73.

36. Jung, *Letters*, 2.257.

37. Jung, *Memories, Dreams, Reflections*, 43.

38. Jung, *CW*, 11.170.

39. Jung, *Memories, Dreams, Reflections*, 93.

40. Ibid., 91.

41. C. G. Jung, *Analytical Psychology: Notes of the Seminar Given in 1925*, ed. W. McGuire (Princeton: Princeton University Press, 1989), 7.
42. Jung, *Memories, Dreams, Reflections*, 94, 91.
43. Jung, *CW*, 10.10–12.
44. Jung, *Memories, Dreams, Reflections*, 40.
45. Jung, *Letters*, 2.257.
46. Jung, *Memories, Dreams, Reflections*, 233.
47. Jung, *Letters*, 2.257–58.
48. Jung, *The Visions Seminars*, 1.156.
49. C. G. Jung, *The Zofingia Lectures*, ed. W. McGuire (Princeton: Princeton University Press, 1983), xiii; Gerhard Wehr, *Jung: A Biography*, trans. D. M. Weeks (Boston: Shambhala Publications, Inc., 1988), 58.
50. Wehr tells of "Jung's ability to fascinate his colleagues in lectures of all sorts . . . on the most controversial topics possible," e.g., "On the Limits of Exact Science" or "The Value of Speculative Research" (Wehr, *Jung*, 59–60).
51. Jung, *Memories, Dreams, Reflections*, 97.
52. Nathan Schwartz-Salant, "Patriarchy in Transformation: Judaic, Christian, and Clinical Perspectives," *Jung's Challenge to Contemporary Religion*, ed. M. Stein and R. L. Moore (Wilmette, Ill: Chiron Publications, 1987), 64.
53. Jung, *Letters*, 2.116.
54. Ibid., 17–18, 20.
55. Jung, *CW*, 11.559.
56. Ibid., 357, in prefatory note preceding par. 553.
57. Wehr, *Jung*, 392–3.
58. Ibid., 382.
59. Jung, *Memories, Dreams, Reflections*, 92.
60. Two entries that exceed "Bible" in column size are "Animals" (36 columns) and "Alchemical Writers and Texts" (27).
61. Jung, *Letters*, 2.424 (italics added).
62. Jung, *Memories, Dreams, Reflections*, 181–82; *Analytical Psychology*, 63–64.
63. Jung, *Analytical Psychology*, 88–90, 92–99.
64. Jung, *Memories, Dreams, Reflections*, 216–17.
65. Ibid., 217–18.
66. Ibid., 219–20.
67. Ibid., 213.
68. Ibid., 214. Jung's sense that he was taking over his father's unfinished business is suggested in two dreams of Jung six weeks after his father's death, in which his father returns and Jung is concerned that he might "be annoyed with me for having moved into his room" (96).
69. Ibid., 213.
70. Ibid., 216.
71. Ibid., 215.
72. Murray Stein, *Jung's Treatment of Christianity: The Psychotherapy of a Religious Tradition* (Wilmette, Ill: Chiron Publications, 1985), 1–19; cf. esp. 17.

73. James E. Dittes, "Analytical (Jungian) Psychology and Religion," in *Dictionary of Pastoral Care and Counseling*, ed. R. J. Hunter (Nashville: Abingdon, 1990), 34–34.

74. Peter Homans, "Psychology and Hermeneutics: Jung's Contribution," *Zygon* 4/4 (1969): 349.

75. Jung, *CW*, 11.1.

76. Ibid., 15.132–33.

77. Ibid., 133.

78. Ibid., 13.73.

79. Ibid., 11.749 n2.

80. Ibid., 15.97–8.

81. Ibid., 162, 156.

82. C. G. Jung, *Psychological Reflections*, ed. J. Jacobi and R. F. C. Hull (Princeton: Princeton University Press, 1978), 342 (from multigraphed copies of Jung's Basel seminar, 1934).

83. Jung, *CW*, 15.134.

84. Ibid., 125.

85. Ibid., 135.

86. Jung, *Letters*, 2.75.

87. Jung, *CW*, 15.160.

88. Ibid., 131.

89. Ibid., 105.

90. Ibid., 130.

91. Ibid., 12.18.

92. Ibid., 9.ii.79.

93. Wilhelm Wuellner cites the description of "rhetorical study" by W. Booth, as "the study of use, of purpose pursued, targets hit or missed, practices illuminated for the sake not of pure knowledge, but of further (and improved) practice" ("Where is Rhetorical Criticism Taking us?" *The Catholic Biblical Quarterly* 49 [1987]: 449).

94. Much in the same way a newspaper editorial or political commentary by a seasoned hand might venture a judgment on a public figure solely on the basis of what that person has written and said, and not be far off the mark, though without final proof.

95. Bernhard Anderson, *Understanding the Old Testament* (Englewood Cliffs, N.J.: Prentice Hall, 1986), 429. See: David Halperin, *Seeking Ezekiel: Text and Psychology* (University Park: Pennsylvania State University Press, 1993).

96. Jung, *CW*, 4.783.

97. Ibid., 10.367.

98. Ibid., 11.696 n6.

99. Ibid., 9.ii.276.

100. Edward F. Edinger, *The Bible and the Psyche: Individuation Symbolism in the Old Testament* (Toronto: Inner City Books, 1986), 13.

101. Jung, *CW*, 13.74.

102. Ibid., 11.148.

103. Jung, *Letters*, 2.76–77.

104. Jung, *CW*, 12.15.

105. Jolande Jacobi, *The Psychology of C. G. Jung* (New Haven: Yale University Press, 1971), 86.

106. Jung, *CW*, 10.443.
107. Ibid., 15.161.
108. Ibid., 73–119.
109. In the United States the San Francisco based Guild for Psychological Studies, founded by Dr. Elizabeth Boyden Howes and Dr. Sheila Moon, were among the first to develop the method to interpret the life and teachings of Jesus. Walter Wink elaborates on the basics of this approach in his *Transforming Bible Study* (Nashville: Abingdon, 110), integrating a Jungian hermeneutic method with classical biblical scholarship.
110. Morris Philipson, *Outline of a Jungian Aesthetics* (Evanston: Northwestern University Press, 1963), 62.
111. Janet Dallett, "Active Imagination in Practice," in *Jungian Analysis*, ed. M. Stein (Boston: New Science Library, 1982), 174.
112. Homans, "Psychology and Hermeneutics," 345.
113. Jung, *CW*, 8.180.
114. Dallet, "Active Imagination in Practice," 176.
115. Jung, *Memories, Dreams, Reflections*, 326.

1 Jacob—A Study in Individuation

1. C. G. Jung, *CW*, 7.102 (see the bibliography entry at the end of the book for an explanation of the manner of notation of the *Collected Works* of Jung).
2. Ibid., 219; cf. *CW*, 9.i.136.
3. C. G. Jung and M.-L. von Franz, eds., *Man and His Symbols* (Garden City: Doubleday, 1964), 67. It is important to note Jung's particular use of the term *archetype* in contrast to that of others such as T. H. Gaster, B. Malinowski, M. Eliade, and C. Levi-Strauss, which refer to the content of images, rather than to their formation (Cf. R. J. Z. Werblowsky, "Structure and Archetypes," *Journal of the Ancient Near Eastern Society of Columbia University* 5 [1973]: 435–442).
4. Jung, *CW*, 9.i.121.
5. Ibid., 8.325.
6. Ibid., 15.137.
7. Ibid., 136, 143.
8. Jung and von Franz, *Man and his Symbols*, 168, 118.
9. Jesus' parable about seeing the speck in another's eye while bearing a log in one's own is a warning against projecting the shadow.
10. Jung, *CW*, 7.314. The corresponding archetype in women is the *animus*. Jung develops the concept of the anima much more fully than the animus, and the animus is not germane to the present study. Some significant questions about Jung's formulation of archetypes are coming from feminist critics (Cf. Naomi Goldenberg, "Jung after Feminism," in *Beyond Androcentrism: New Essays on Women and Religion*, ed. R. M. Gross, American Academy of Religion Aids for the Study of Religion 6 [Missoula: Scholars Press, 1977], 53–66).
11. Jung, *CW*, 7.317.
12. Ibid., 9.i.66.
13. Ibid., 56.

14. Ibid., 7.464.
15. Jung and von Franz, *Man and his Symbols*, 162.
16. Ibid., 202.
17. Jung, *CW*, 9.i.490.
18. June Singer, *Boundaries of the Soul: The Practice of Jung's Psychology* (Garden City: Doubleday, 1972), 140.
19. This formulation of individuation is taken from: Jolande Jacobi, *The Way of Individuation*, trans. R. F. C. Hull (New York: Harcourt, Brace, and World, 1967), 34–48.
20. Jung, *CW*, 7.382.
21. Jung and von Franz, *Man and his Symbols*, 216.
22. Jacobi, *The Way of Individuation*, 42.
23. See the brief survey of the history of interpretation in: Ronald S. Hendel, *The Epic of the Patriarch: The Jacob Cycle and the Narrative Traditions of Caanan and Israel*, Harvard Semitic Monographs 42 (Atlanta: Scholar's Press, 1987), 1–32.
24. David J. A. Clines, *The Theme of the Pentateuch*, Journal for the Study of the Old Testament Supplement Series 10 (Sheffield: University of Sheffield, 1982), 29.
25. Michael Fishbane, *Text and Texture* (New York: Schocken, 1979), 42.
26. J. P. Fokkelman, "Genesis," in *The Literary Guide to the Bible*, ed. R. Alter and F. Kermode (Cambridge: Harvard University Press, 1987), 46–47, 50–52.
27. These sections serve to link the Jacob cycle with the preceding stories about Abraham and subsequent relations with the inhabitants of Canaan. They do not deal specifically with Jacob's development.
28. Athalya Brenner, "Female Social Behavior: Two Descriptive Patterns Within the 'Birth of the Hero' Paradigm," *Vetus Testamentum*, 1986: 258; Ronald S. Hendel, *The Epic of the Patriarch: The Jacob Cycle and the Narrative Traditions of Caanan and Israel*, Harvard Semitic Monographs 42 (Atlanta: Scholar's, 1987), 39–58, 140. Other biblical heroes with "barren" mothers include Samson (Judg. 13:2–24), Samuel (I Sam. 1:1–20), and John the Baptizer (Luke1:7–25).
29. Jung, *CW*, 9.i.282; cf. Joseph Campbell, *The Hero With a Thousand Faces* (Princeton: Princeton University Press, 1973). Moses' escape from death at birth (Exodus 2:1–10) and Jesus' birth to a virgin (Matt. 1:18–25; Luke 1:26–38), as well as escape from Herod (Matt. 2:13–18) are other expressions of the archetype.
30. Erich Neumann, *The Origins and History of Consciousness* (Princeton: Princeton University Press,1971), 95; Heinz Westman, *The Structure of Biblical Myths: the Ontogenesis of the Psyche* (Dallas: Spring Publications, 1983), 333.
31. C. G. Jung and M. L. von Franz, *Man and his Symbols*, 113; cf. Robert Graves and Raphael Patai, *Hebrew Myths: The Book of Genesis* (Garden City: Doubleday, 1964), 190–91.
32. Neumann, *The Origins and History of Consciousness*, 272.
33. Ibid., 298.
34. Christa Meves, *The Bible Answers Us with Pictures*, trans. H. Taussig (Philadelphia: Westminster, 1977), 73–74.
35. Jung and von Franz, *Man and his Symbols*, 118.

36. Jung, *CW*, 7.314.
37. Ibid., 9.i.64.
38. John A. Sanford, *The Man Who Wrestled with God: A Study of Individuation* (King of Prussia: Religious Publishing, 1974), 24.
39. We might wonder what part Isaac may have played in the deception. Gunther Plaut notes, "consciously, Isaac cannot admit to knowing the identity of Jacob in v. 23; subconsciously, he is relieved" (*The Torah: A Modern Commentary*. vol. I, *Genesis* [New York: Union of American Hebrew Congregations, 1974], 274). As the Father who passes on the *birakah* from God, does he recognize in Jacob the necessary qualities to carry on the family line?
40. Christa Meves, *The Bible Answers Us with Pictures*, 74.
41. J. Kühlewein, "Gotteserfahrung und Reifungsgeschichte in der Jakob-Esau-Erzählung," *Werden und Wirken des Alten Testaments: Festschrift für Claus Westermann zum 70. Geburtstag*, ed. R. Albertz, Hans-Peter Mueller, Hans Walter Wolff, and Walther Zimmerli (Göttingen: Vandenhoeck and Ruprecht, 1980), 118.
42. Campbell, *Hero with a Thousand Faces*, 78.
43. Graves and Patai, *Hebrew Myths*, 205, 208.
44. Hendel, *The Epic of the Patriarch*, 63.
45. Campbell, *Hero with a Thousand Faces*, 69.
46. Hendel, *The Epic of the Patriarch*, 64.
47. Bruce Vawter, *On Genesis: A New Reading* (Garden City: Doubleday, 1977), 312. Brown, Driver, Briggs considers the word to derive from the root *sll*, meaning "to lift or cast up" (699–700).
48. E. Speiser, *Genesis*, Anchor Bible, vol. 1 (Garden City: Doubleday, 1964), 219. Bruce Vawter suggests that the naturally terraced topography of Beth-el might have suggested the image (*A Path Through Genesis* [New York: Sheed and Ward, 1956], 201).
49. Mircea Eliade, *Patterns in Comparative Religion*, trans. R. Sheed (New York: Sheed and Ward, 1958), 108.
50. Mircea Eliade, *Shamanism: Archaic Techniques of Ecstasy*, trans. W. Trask (London: Routledge and Kegan Paul, 1964), 110–44.
51. Eliade, *Shamanism*, 134; Robert Davidson, *Genesis 12–50* (Cambridge: University Press, 1979), 146.
52. Charles B. Chavel, *Ramban (Nachmanides) Commentary on the Torah: Genesis* (New York: Shilo, 1971), 350–57.
53. Elie Wiesel, *Messengers of God* (New York: Random House, 1976), 113.
54. Edward Edinger, *The Bible and the Psyche: Individuation Symbolism in the Old Testament* (Toronto: Inner City Books, 1986), 38; cf. *Ego and Archetype: Individuation and the Religious Function of the Psyche* (New York: G.P. Putnam's Sons, 1972), 69–71.
55. John Sanford, *The Man who Wrestled with God*, 32; J. Kühlewein, "Gotteserfahrung und Reifungsgeschichte," 121.
56. C. G. Jung, *CW*, 9.ii.305; *CW*, 8.405.
57. John Sanford, *The Man who Wrestled with God*, 33.
58. Rabbinic commentators tried to mitigate the seeming crassness of the bargain. Ramban notes that '*im* here may not be conditional, but simply referring to future events. See: Plaut, *The Torah*, 282, 358.
59. Campbell, *Hero with a Thousand Faces*, 97.

60. Jung and von Franz, *Man and his Symbols*, 180, 185–86.
61. Sanford, *The Man who Wrestled with God*, 35.
62. Kühlewein, "Gotteserfahrung und Reifungsgeschichte," 119.
63. Martin Buber, "Darko shel miqra'," in *The Hebrew Bible in Literary Criticism*, ed. A. Preminger and E. Greenstein (New York: Ungar, 1986), 428.
64. Meves, *The Bible Answers Us with Pictures*, 74; Sanford, *The Man who Wrestled with God*, 39.
65. Kühlewein, "Gotteserfahrung und Reifungsgeschichte," 118; Sanford, *The Man who Wrestled with God*, 42.
66. Kühlewein, "Gotteserfahrung und Reifungsgeschichte," 119.
67. H. N. Strickman and Arthur M. Silver, eds., *Ibn Ezra's Commentary on the Pentateuch: Genesis (Bereshit)* (New York: Menorah, 1988), 310; Chavel, *Ramban*, 392.
68. Speiser, *Genesis*, 256.
69. Kühlewein, "Gotteserfahrung und Reifungsgeschichte," 116.
70. Meves, *The Bible Answers Us with Pictures*, 76.
71. Kühlewein, "Gotteserfahrung und Reifungsgeschichte," 119. Roland Barthes comments at length on the way the narrative structure here is "intertwined" and ambiguous ("The Struggle with the Angel: Textual Analysis of Genesis 32:23–33," in *Structural Analysis and Biblical Exegesis*, ed. F. Bovon, et. al., [Pittsburgh: Pickwick, 1974], 24ff).
72. Meves, *The Bible Answers us with Pictures*, 77; Kühlewein, "Gotteserfahrung und Reifungsgeschichte," 122.
73. Sanford, *The Man who Wrestled with God*, 44; Kühlewein, "Gotteserfahrung und Reifungsgeschichte," 122.
74. Vawter, *On Genesis*, 349.
75. Wiesel, *Messengers of God*, 107.
76. William T. Miller, *Mysterious Encounters at Mamre and Jabbok*, Brown Judaic Studies 50, ed. J. Neusner (Chico: Scholars Press, 1984), 98.
77. Miller, *Mysterious Encounters*, 102; Chavel, *Ramban*, 359.
78. Miller, *Mysterious Encounters*, 114.
79. H. Strickman and A. Silver, eds., *Ibn Ezra's Commentary*, 318 (Ibn Ezra refers the reader to Exod. 23:21 for "enlightenment").
80. Fishbane, *Text and Texture*, 52–53.
81. Miller, *Mysterious Encounters*, 114.
82. Davidson, *Genesis 12–50* (Cambridge: University Press, 1979), 185; Vawter, *On Genesis*, 349; Plaut, *The Torah*, 324. Walter Wink remarks that "even if it were a water spirit, the story deserves to be taken at least seriously enough to ask what symbolic, psychic, or mythological content might be coming to expression through such a figure" ("On Wrestling with God: Using Psychological Insights in Biblical Study," in *Religion in Life* 47 (1978):137).
83. Hendel, *The Epic of the Patriarch*, 105.
84. Wiesel, *Messengers of God*, 124.
85. Fishbane, *Text and Texture*, 53.
86. Plaut, *The Torah*, 324. Cf. Wink "to focus only on [personal] psychological aspects of the narrative" is to strip "it of its religious depth" ("On Wrestling with God," 138).

87. Jung, *CW*, 9.ii.351–56.
88. Ibid., 115–17; Edinger, *Ego and Archetype*, 132.
89. Jung, *CW*, 5.524.
90. Sanford, *The Man who Wrestled with God*, 46.
91. Meves, *The Bible Answers Us with Pictures*, 77.
92. Kühlewein, "Gotteserfahrung und Reifungsgeschichte," 125.
93. Buber, "Darko shel miqra," 428.
94. Cf. Speiser's statement, "The question about Jacob's name is rhetorical!" (*Genesis*, 255).
95. Sanford, *The Man who Wrestled with God*, 45; cf. Vawter, *On Genesis*, 351, on the impossibility of naming God.
96. *Genesis Rabbah* 78.4 (Miller, *Mysterious Encounters*, 105); James H. Lowe, ed., *"Rashi" on the Pentateuch: Genesis* (London: Hebrew Compendium Publishing, 1928), 361.
97. Miller, *Mysterious Encounters*, 112.
98. Lowe, *"Rashi,"* 360; Davidson, *Genesis*, 186.
99. Vawter, *On Genesis*, 351; cf. Kühlewein, "Gotteserfahrung und Reifungsgeschichte," 126.
100. Fishbane, *Text and Texture*, 53.
101. Edinger, *Ego and Archetype*, 96.
102. Wiesel, *Messengers of God*, 133.
103. Kühlewein, "Gotteserfahrung und Reifungsgeschichte," 117.
104. Hendel, *The Epic of the Patriarch*, 133–34.
105. Westman, *The Structure of Biblical Myths*, 205.
106. Wink describes the "hourglass" structure of the story by which events are removed from their historical context and projected on the story figure. As we "find ourselves in him, or him in us," those events are returned to history in our own lives ("On Wrestling with God," 144). On ways to approach the archetypal dimensions of stories in the Hebrew scriptures to encourage personal transformation, see: Sadie Gregory, *A New Dimension in Old Testament Study: A Course Guide to the Study of Selections from the Old Testament for Individuals and Groups* (San Francisco: Guild for Psychological Studies, 1980); Conrad L'Heureux, *Life Journey and the Old Testament: An Experiential Approach to the Bible and Personal Transformation* (New York: Paulist, 1986); and, Walter Wink, *Transforming Bible Study: A Leader's Guide* (Nashville: Abingdon, 1980).

2 Joseph's Dreams

1. Elie Wiesel, *Messengers of God* (New York: Summit Books, 1976), 141.
2. Nahum M. Sarna, *Understanding Genesis* (New York: Schocken Books, 1966), 211.
3. Dorothy Zeligs, *Psychoanalysis and the Bible* (New York: Bloch Publishing Company, 1974), 89–90.
4. Ibid., 90.
5. W. Clark Falconer and Colin A. Ross, "The Tilted Family," *Canadian Journal of Psychiatry* 31/7 (1986): 649–52.
6. Sarna, *Understanding Genesis*, 212.

7. Zeligs, *Psychoanalysis and the Bible*, 64.
8. Sarna, *Understanding Genesis*, 213.
9. Falconer and Ross, "The Tilted Family," 649.
10. John Sanford, *King Saul, The Tragic Hero* (New York: Paulist Press, 1985), 132–34.
11. Wiesel, *Messengers of God*, 165.
12. Sanford, *King Saul*, 108.
13. Zeligs, *Psychoanalysis and the Bible*, 78.
14. Ibid., 90.
15. Gerhard von Rad, "The Joseph Narrative and Ancient Wisdom," in *The Problem of the Hexateuch* (New York: McGraw Hill, 1966), 293–300.
16. Wisdom of Amenemope 19.16, in Gerhard von Rad, "The Joseph Narrative," 297.
17. Ibid., 299.

3 Johannine Symbolism

1. Xavier Leon-Dufour, "Towards a Symbolic Reading of the Fourth Gospel," *NTS* 27 (1980–81): 439–56.
2. Ibid., 440.
3. Ibid., 441.
4. Rudolf Bultmann, *The Gospel of John: A Commentary*, tr. G. R. Beasley-Murray, et al. (Philadelphia: Westminster, 1971), 41.
5. John Painter, "Johannine Symbols: A Case Study in Epistemology," *Journal of Theology for Southern Africa* 27 (1979): 26–41.
6. Ibid., 40.
7. Ibid., 34.
8. Cf. Bengt Holmberg, *Sociology and the New Testament: An Appraisal* (Minneapolis: Fortress, 1990); Bruce Malina, *The New Testament World: A Cultural Anthropological Approach* (Atlanta: John Knox, 1981).
9. Robin Scroggs, "The Sociological Interpretation of the New Testament: The Present State of Research," *NTS* 26 (1980): 166.
10. George MacRae, "The Fourth Gospel and Religionsgeschichte," *CBQ* 32 (1970): 13–24.
11. Wayne Meeks, "The Man from Heaven in Johannine Sectarianism," *JBL* 91 (1972): 44–72. Cf. also Jerome R. Neyrey, *An Ideology of Revolt: Johannine Christology in Social-Science Perspective* (Philadelphia: Fortress, 1988).
12. Craig Koester, "Symbol and Unity in the Fourth Gospel," paper presented at the Upper Midwest SBL meeting in March 1989 and at the CBA meeting in August 1989. I am indebted to Dr. Koester for graciously sharing a copy of this paper with me. He is pursuing this kind of approach in a forthcoming book on the symbols in the Fourth Gospel to be published by Fortress.
13. Murray Krieger, *A Window to Criticism: Shakespeare's Sonnets and Modern Poetics* (Princeton: Princeton, 1964), 3–4.
14. Cf. Stephen D. Moore, *Literary Criticism and the Gospels: The Theoretical Challenge* (New Haven: Yale University Press, 1989).
15. R. Alan Culpepper, *Anatomy of the Fourth Gospel: A Study in Literary Design* (Philadelphia: Fortress, 1983), 180–198.

16. Ibid., 188–189.
17. His category of "core symbols" was derived from Edward K. Brown, *Rhythm in the Novel* (Toronto: University of Toronto), 55–59.
18. Robert Kysar, "Johannine Metaphor—Meaning and Function: A Literary Case Study of John 10:1–8," *Semeia* 53 (1991): 81–111.
19. Ibid., 95–96.
20. Ibid., 98, 100.
21. Wilhelm Wuellner, "Putting Life back into the Lazarus Story," *Semeia* 53 (1991): 119.
22. Moore, *Literary Criticism*, 95–98, 106–107.
23. Much the same point is made by Robin Scroggs, "Psychology as a Tool to Interpret the Text," *Christian Century* (March 24, 1982): 335–36.
24. Gerd Theissen, *Psychological Aspects of Pauline Theology* (Philadelphia: Fortress, 1987), 1.
25. Walter Wink, *Naming the Powers: The Language of Power in the New Testament* (Philadelphia: Fortress, 1984); *Unmasking the Powers: The Invisible Forces that Determine Human Existence* (Philadelphia: Fortress, 1986); *Engaging the Powers: Discernment and Resistance in a World of Domination* (Minneapolis: Fortress, 1992).
26. Walter Wink, *The Bible in Human Transformation: Toward a New Paradigm for Biblical Study* (Philadelphia: Fortress, 1973).
27. Walter Wink, "On Wrestling with God: Using Psychological Insights in Biblical Study," *Religion in Life* 47 (1978): 141. Cf. also his *Transforming Bible Study: A Leader's Guide* (Nashville: Abingdon, 1989), for a practical guide in leading groups in this sort of Bible study.
28. Rollins, *Jung and the Bible* (Atlanta: John Knox, 1983); "Jung on Scripture and Hermeneutics: Retrospect and Project," *Essays on Jung and the Study of Religion*, eds. L. H. Martin and J. Goss (New York: University Press of America, 1985), 81–94; "Jung's Challenge to Biblical Hermeneutics," *Jung's Challenge to Contemporary Religion*, ed. M. Stein and R. Moore (Wilmette: Chiron Publications, 1986) .
29. Schuyler Brown, "The Beloved Disciple: A Jungian View," *The Conversation Continues: Studies in Paul and John in Honor of J. Louis Martyn*, ed. R. T. Fortna and B. R. Gaventa (Nashville: Abingdon, 1990): 366–377; "Universalism and Particularism in Matthew's Gospel," *SBL Seminar Papers*, ed. D. J. Lull (Atlanta: Scholars Press, 1989): 388–399.
30. Michael E. Willett, "Jung and John," *Explorations* 77 (Fall 1988): 77–92.
31. Paul Diel and Jeannine Solotareff, *Symbolism in the Gospel of John* (San Francisco: Harper and Row, 1988). Diel died in 1972, and the book was prepared by his student Solotareff, based on manuscripts written by Diel over 40 years ago. Diel's interest in biblical symbolism is evident in his other books, *The God-Symbol* (San Francisco: Harper and Row, 1986) and *Symbolism in the Bible* (San Francisco: Harper and Row, 1986).
32. Diel and Solotareff, *Symbolism in the Gospel of John*, 1.
33. Cf. Stephen Neill, *The Interpretation of the New Testament 1861–1961* (London: Oxford University Press, 1964), esp. chap. 1, "Challenge to Orthodoxy," 1–32.

34. Diel and Solotareff, *Symbolism in the Gospel of John*, 25.

35. Ibid., 52 (authors' emphasis).

36. Ibid., 77–78.

37. C. G. Jung, *CW*, 5 (see bibliography entry at the end of the book for an explanation of the manner of notation of the *Collected Works* of Jung).

38. C. G. Jung, et al., *Man and his Symbols* (New York: Dell, 1964).

39. Jung, *CW*, 11.746.

40. Cf. Wallace B. Clift's chapter 7, "The Uniting Quality of Symbols," in his *Jung and Christianity: The Challenge of Reconciliation* (New York: Crossroad, 1982), 51–57.

41. Cf. C. G. Jung, "The Transcendent Function," in *CW*, 8.131–93.

42. C. G. Jung, "Symbols and the Interpretation of Dreams," in *CW*, 18.482. In this respect Jung's conception of symbols was very similar to that of Paul Tillich. For a study of the two, cf. John P. Dourley, *The Psyche as Sacrament: A Comparative Study of C. G. Jung and Paul Tillich* (Toronto: Inner City, 1981), esp. 31–47 on symbols.

43. Cf. C. G. Jung, "The Archetypes and the Collective Unconscious," in *CW*, 9.i.1–86.

44. Cf.C. G. Jung, "The Shadow," in *CW*, 9.ii.13–19.

45. Cf. C. G. Jung, "The Syzygy: Anima and Animus," in *CW*, 9.ii.20–42.

46. Cf. C. G. Jung, "The Self," in *CW*, 9.ii.43–67.

47. Jung, *CW*, 11.757.

48. C. G. Jung, "Symbols and the Interpretation of Dreams," in *CW*, 18.431.

49. Cf. C. G. Jung, *CW*, 18, esp. the second half of Tavistock Lecture 5, 391–415.

50. Jung, *CW*, 18.434.

51. Ibid.,483.

52. Ibid., 521.

53. C. G. Jung, "The Practical Use of Dream Analysis," in *CW*, 16.330.

54. C. G. Jung, "Psychology and Literature," in *CW*, 15.133. Cf. also his "On the Relation of Analytical Psychology to Poetry," in *CW*, 15.97–132.

55. Jung, *CW*, 15.140–44.

56. Ibid., 5.48.

57. Ibid., 15.153.

58. Cf. Michael E. Willett, *Wisdom Christology in the Fourth Gospel* (San Francisco: Mellen Research University Press, 1992), 57–58, 100.

59. For a similar approach, cf. Wink, *Naming the Powers*, 118–148, where he wrote, "Heaven is the transcendent 'within' of material reality" (118). Cf. also Jung's own interpretation of the Gnostic myths, in which he equated divinity with the unconscious and matter with the ego. See: C. G. Jung, "Gnostic Symbols of the Self," in *CW*, 9.ii.287–346.

60. Painter, "Johannine Symbols," 35 (author's emphasis).

61. C. G. Jung, "Christ, A Symbol of the Self," in *CW*, 9.ii.68–126.

62. Cf. Elisabeth Schussler Fiorenza, *In Memory of Her: A Feminist Theological Reconstruction* (New York: Crossroad, 1984), 323–33. Cf. also Willett, *Wisdom Christology*, 145–47, and the literature cited on 145 n.70.

63. Cf. Culpepper, *Anatomy of the Fourth Gospel*, 146–48, listing seven responses which characters made toward Jesus in the Gospel narrative.
64. Cf. Willett, *Wisdom Christology*, 102–103.
65. The important study in this regard is J. Louis Martyn, *History and Theology in the Fourth Gospel* (Nashville: Abingdon, 1979). Martyn contended that the Johannine Christians were expelled from the synagogue based on the "Benediction Against Heretics," which had recently been introduced in the synagogue liturgy. The Gospel, then, was written as a "two-level" drama, in which Jesus' struggle against the Jews reflected the struggle of the Johannine community against the synagogue authorities. Recently scholars have questioned whether the "Benediction Against Heretics" was the specific instrument by which Johannine Christians were excluded from the synagogue. There is, however, widespread agreement that whatever the instrument, the group was in fact excluded. Cf. David Rensberger, *Johannine Faith and Liberating Community* (Philadelphia: Westminster, 1987), 26.
66. Rensberger, *Johannine Faith*, 26–27.
67. Cf. C. G. Jung, "The Shadow," in *CW*, 9.ii.16–17.
68. Cf. Raymond E. Brown, *The Community of the Beloved Disciple* (New York: Paulist, 1979), 103–9; cf. also his *The Epistles of John*, Anchor Bible 30 (Garden City, N.Y.: Doubleday, 1981), 69–115.
69. Brown, *Community of the Beloved Disciple*, 145–167.
70. Mary Ann Tolbert, "A Response from a Literary Perspective," *Semeia* 53 (1991), 206.
71. Fernando F. Segovia, "Towards a New Direction in Johannine Scholarship: The Fourth Gospel from a Literary Perspective," *Semeia* 53 (1991), 16–17.
72. C. G. Jung, "Christ as Symbol of the Self," in *CW*, 9.ii.74–75. Cf. also his "A Psychological Approach to the Trinity," in *CW*, 11.232.
73. Segovia, "The Final Farewell of Jesus: A Reading of John 20:30–21:25," *Semeia* 53 (1991), 187–188.
74. David L. Miller, *Christs: Meditations on Archetypal Images in Christian Theology* (New York: Seabury, 1981), 11–19.
75. David Miller, *Christs*, 28–43.
76. I am grateful to those who have read and commented on various stages of this essay: Walter Wink, Lucy Sikes, Tom Peterson, and Richard Sugg.

4 The Myth of Sophia

1. For an account of the discovery of these texts, see K. Rudolph, *Gnosis: The Nature and History of Gnosticism*, trans. R. M. Wilson (New York: Harper and Row, 1987), 34–52.
2. I have avoided the English neologism "Gnosticism," which has no equivalent in German scholarship, since the distinction between Gnosis and Gnosticism involves some questionable assumptions. Cf. J. M. Robinson, "The Messina Definition of Gnosticism," in "On Bridging the Gulf from Q to the Gospel of Thomas (or vice versa)," in

Nag Hammadi, Gnosticism, and Early Christianity, ed. C. W. Hedrick and R. Hodgson, Jr. (Peabody: Hendrickson Publishers, 1986), 128–35.

3. C. G. Jung, *CW*, 9.ii (see the bibliography-entry at the end of the book for an explanation of the manner of notation of the *Collected Works* of Jung).

4. *The Gospel According to Thomas: Coptic Text*. Established and Trans. A. Guillaumont, et al. (New York: Harper and Row, 1959).

5. Professor Gilles Quispel has informed me through a mutual acquaintance, Ms. Barbara Miller, that he visited Jung in Küsnacht shortly after the discovery of the Nag Hammadi Library in 1945 and explained to him the significance of the new material.

6. This source material included the testimony of the heresiologists, especially Irenaeus, Hippolytus, and Epiphanius; Clement of Alexandria and Origen; the Gnostic texts which were known before 1945, especially the *Pistis Sophia*, Berlin Papyrus 8502, the *Two Books of Jeu*, and the apocryphal Acts.

7. The "history of traditions" approach to the Bible was introduced into Old Testament studies by Hermann Gunkel and applied to the New Testament by Rudolf Bultmann and Martin Dibelius. It is congenial to the Lutheran emphasis on "justification by faith," which prefers the inner history of ideas to the outer history of events. See R. Morgan and J. Barton, *Biblical Interpretation* (Oxford University Press, 1988), 96–124.

8. Jung, *CW*, 9.ii.428.

9. C. G. Jung, *Memories, Dreams, and Reflections*, trans. R. and C. Winston (New York: Vintage Books, 1963), 38.

10. From "A History of *Lulu*," by Karen Monson, reprinted in the Canadian Opera Company's program notes, courtesy of the Lyric Opera of Chicago and the estate of the author.

11. Jung, *CW*, 9.i.62. Cf. Marlene Dietrich's famous role in the film, "The Blue Angel."

12. June Singer, *Androgyny: Towards a New Theory of Sexuality* (Garden City: Anchor Press/Doubleday, 1977).

13. Joan Englesman, *The Feminine Dimension of the Divine* (Philadelphia: Westminster Press, 1979).

14. Jung, *CW*, 9.i.64.

15. For the Simonian version of the Sophia myth see: G. Lüdemann, *Untersuchungen zur simonianischen Gnosis* (Göttingen: Vandenhoeck and Ruprecht, 1975).

16. Jung, *CW*, 9.i.64.

17. According to Koehler-Baumgartner, *Lexicon in Veteris Testamenti Libros* (Leiden: Brill, 1953), *qnh*, the verb used in Proverbs 8:22, can mean either "acquire" or "create." *Rēshīt* derived from *rōsh*, "head," has the basic meaning "what is first," either in the sense of "beginning" or of "point of departure." W. Kingsland (*The Gnosis or Ancient Wisdom in the Christian Scriptures* [London: Allen and Unwin, 1954], 115) argues against the former translation: "Now in using the word *Beginning* we are introducing the concept of *time*; and time, like space also, is part of that mind-created illusion

which, in our present consciousness, takes the form of an objective world." M.-L. von Franz (*Alchemy: An Introduction to the Symbolism and the Psychology* [Toronto: Inner City Books, 1980], 184) provides evidence that the translation "archetype" is not anachronistic: "The third explanation, which to my mind is the most interesting is that she [Wisdom] represents the sum of all archetypes—this is medieval language, I am not projecting Jungian words—the *archetypi*, or the eternal ideas in God's mind when He created the world."

18. M.-L. von Franz, *Alchemy*, 183.
19. Louis Haartman and P. van Imschoot, "Wisdom," in *Encyclopedic Dictionary of the Bible* (New York: McGraw Hill, 1963), 2587.
20. Jung, *CW*, 9.i.65.
21. John P. Dourley, "The Jung, Buber, White exchanges: Exercises in Futility," *Studies in Religion*, 20 (1991): 301.
22. Used with the author's permission.
23. Richard Smith ("Afterward: The Modern Relevance of Gnosticism," *The Nag Hammadi Library*, ed. J.M. Robinson [San Francisco: Harper and Row, 1988], 547–8) notes: "In 1982, in *Agon*, [Harold] Bloom 'misread' his gnostic precursors and claimed them for the latest school of literary criticism: 'Gnosticism was the inaugural and most powerful of Deconstructions because it undid all genealogies, scrambled all hierarchies, allegorized every microcosm/macrocosm relation, and rejected every representation of divinity as non-referential.'"
24. This seems to be the misapprehension of Robert A. Segal, "Jung and Gnosticism," *Religion*, 17 (1987): 301–36. Jung was not so naive as to suppose that "Gnosticism espouses individuation."
25. *CW*, 5.190–250.
26. *Apocryphon of John, NHC* II, 9:28–30.
27. *Gospel of Philip, NHC* II, 68:22–26.
28. Ibid., 69:24–25.
29. For the sacrament of the Bridal Chamber, see: Rudolph, *Gnosis*, 245–47.
30. *Gospel of Philip, NHC* II, 59:2–3.
31. Peter Brown, *The Body and Society: Men, Women and Sexual Renunciation in Early Christianity* (New York: Columbia University Press, 1988), chap. 5, "'When You Make the Two One': Valentinus and Gnostic Spiritual Guidance," 120.
32. The motif of remembrance finds expression in "The Hymn of the Pearl," from the *Acts of Thomas*. The king's son, upon arriving in Egypt, falls into forgetfulness and receives a letter from home with the summons: "Remember that though you are the son of kings, you have fallen under a servile yoke" (110: 44). The *Gospel of Truth* refers to "disturbing dreams" (*NHC* I, 29: 10) from which one awakes through Gnosis (30: 10).
33. For such a summary, see Rudolph, *Gnosis*, 71–84.
34. *The Thunder, Perfect Mind, NHC* VI, 13: 16–22.
35. Ibid., VI, 14: 9–13.
36. Ibid., 26–31.

37. "Bridal Mysticism in Origen and 'The Exegesis on the Soul'" (unpublished paper).

38. "The Gnostic Myth of Sophia: Then and Now" (unpublished paper).

Afterword

1. C. G. Jung, *CW*, 18.1461 (see bibliography entry at the end of the book for an explanation of the manner of notation of the *Collected Works* of Jung).

2. Henry Corbin, "*Mundus Imaginalis*, or The Imaginary and the Imaginal," *Spring (1972)*; "Pour une charte de l'Imaginal," *Corps spirituel et Terre céleste* (Paris: Editions Buchet/Chastel, 1979), 7–19; and, *Creative Imagination in the Sufism of Ibn 'Arabî*, trans. R. Manheim (London: Routledge and Kegan Paul, 1970), 240.

3. Cf. David L. Miller, "Theology's Ego/Religion's Soul," *Spring* (1980): 78–88.

4. C. G. Jung, *The Visions Seminar*, ed. M. Foote (Zürich: Spring, 1976), I.156.

5. Sigmund Freud, *Standard Edition of the Complete Psychological Works*, vol. 20, trans. J. Strachey (London: Hogarth, 1953–1974), 8.

6. Origen, *On First Principles* (New York: Harper, 1966), 3.6.1.

7. C. G. Jung, *Letters*, trans. R. F. C. Hull (Princeton: Princeton University Press, 1973–1975), 2.210–12 (19 January 1955).

8. Mircea Eliade, *Yoga*, trans. W. Trask (New York: Pantheon, 1958), 219–27; *Cosmos and History* (Torchbook edition; New York: Harper, 1959), vii–ix.

9. Plotinus, *Enneads*, 1.ii.2. Cf. David L. Miller, "Life-likeness and Unlikeness," in *Three Faces of God: Traces of the Trinity in Literature and Life* (Philadelphia: Fortress Press, 1986), 41–51.

10. For example, see: C. G. Jung, *CW*, 18.275, 277, 279; 3.393, 395, 397, 406; 6.8–10.

11. Ibid., 11.460.

12. Ibid., 17.289; 6.705, 757.

13. Ibid., 7.112, 269; "Seminar on Kundalini," *Spring* (1975): 31.

14. James Hillman, *Archetypal Psychology* (Dallas: Spring Publications, 1983), 13.

15. C. G. Jung, *Memories, Dreams, Reflections*, trans. R. and C. Winston (New York: Pantheon, 1963), 205f.

16. C. G. Jung, *Memories, Dreams, Reflections*, 192f.

17. Ibid., 189.

18. C. G. Jung, *Psychological Reflections*, ed. J. Jacobi, trans. R. F. C. Hull (Princeton: Princeton University Press, 1970), 342 (cited from multigraphed copies of Jung's Basel seminar in 1934).

19. J. Z. Smith, *Drudgery Divine* (Chicago: University of Chicago Press, 1990), 38f, citing Burton Mack.

20. J. Z. Smith, *Differential Equations* (Tempe: Arizona State University Department of Religion, 1992), 14.

21. J. Z. Smith, "In Comparison a Magic Dwells," *Imagining Religion* (Chicago: University of Chicago Press, 1982), 35; cf. *Drudgery Divine*, 38f.

22. J. Z. Smith, "Adde parvum parvo magnus acervus erit," *Map is not the Territory* (Leiden: Brill, 1978), 240.
23. Howard Eilberg-Schwartz, *The Savage in Judaism* (Bloomington: University of Indiana Press, 1990), 95.
24. Ibid., 98.
25. Ibid., 99. Cf. Eilberg-Schwartz strong defense of this position in: "Voyeurism, Anthropology, and the Study of Judaism," *Journal of the American Academy of Religion* 62/1 (1994): 173–78.
26. Walter Wink, "On Wrestling with God: Using Psychological Insights in Biblical Study," *Religion in Life* 47 (1978): 141.

❈ CONTRIBUTORS ❈

Schuyler Brown teaches on the Faculty of Theology of St. Michael's College, Toronto, and at the Centre for the Study of Religion of the University of Toronto. Brown was educated at Harvard University, Woodstock College, the University of Muenster, and the Biblical Institute in Rome. He is the author of *Apostasy and Perseverance in the Theology of Luke* and *The Origins of Christianity: A Historical Introduction to the New Testament.* A forthcoming work is *Text and Psyche: The Bible and Religious Experience.*

D. Andrew Kille is working in an interdisciplinary program of Biblical studies and psychology at the Graduate Theological Union in Berkeley. He holds degrees from Stanford University and the American Baptist Seminary of the West. His publications include the article, "Word and Psyche: Intersections of the Psychology of Religion and the Bible" in the journal *Paradigms.*

David L. Miller is Watson-Ledden Professor of Religion at Syracuse University. He was a member of the Eranos Circle in Ascona, Switzerland between the years 1975 and 1988, and is a frequent lecturer at Jung Institutes in Switzerland, Canada, Japan, and the United States. His books include *Christs: Meditations on Archetypal Images in Christan Theology, Three Faces of God,* and *Hells and Holy Ghosts.*

Michael Willett Newheart teaches New Testament literature and language at Howard University School of Divinity in Washington, D.C. He previously taught at three seminaries in the Kansas City area. His recent book is called *Wisdom Christology in the Fourth Gospel,* and he serves as associate editor of "The Bible Workbench," an adult Bible study curriculum utilizing psychological perspectives.

Wayne G. Rollins has been professor of theology and coordinator of the Graduate Program in Theology at Assumption College in Worcester, Massachusetts since 1978. His doctorate is from Yale University, and his earlier teaching positions include Princeton University, Wellesley College, and Hartford Seminary Foundation. He is the author of *The Gospels: Portraits of Christ* and *Jung and the Bible*. A forthcoming work is entitled *The Bible in Psychological Perspective: Retrospect and Prospect.* He is the current chair of the consultation on "Psychology and Biblical Studies" of the Society of Biblical Literature.

Trevor Watt is professor of religious studies at Canisius College where he teaches Psychology of Religion. He is the chair of the "Psychology of Religion" group on the American Academy of Religion and is a fellow at the American Association of Pastoral counselors and a therapist in the Family Clinic at the University of Rochester's Department of Psychiatry.

❧ BIBLIOGRAPHY ❧

The bibliography that follows includes, not only the works referred to in the chapters of this book, but also additional resources in the relation between depth psychology and biblical interpretation.

Anderson, Bernhard. *Understanding the Old Testament.* Englewood Cliffs: Prentice Hall, 1986.

Auchter, Thomas. "Zum Schuldverstandnis in der Psychoanalyse im Alten und Neuen Testament." *Wege zum Menschen* 30 (1978): 208–25.

Barande, I. "Das Verbrechen an Moses ersetzt den Todestrieb." *Jahrbuch der Psychoanalyse* 21 (1987), 13–30.

Barth, Hans Martin. "Gottes Wort ist dreifaltig: ein Beitrag zur Auseinandersetzung mit der 'archetypischen Hermeneutik' Eugen Drewermanns." *Theologische Literaturzeitung* 113 (1988): 244–54.

Barthes, Roland. "The Struggle with the Angel: Textual Analysis of Genesis 32:23–33." In *Structural Analysis and Biblical Exegesis,* ed. Francis Bovon, et. al., 21–33. Pittsburgh: Pickwick, 1974.

Berguer, George. *Some Aspects of the Life of Jesus: From the Psychological and Psycho-Analytic Point of View.* Trans. E. S. and V. Brooks. New York: Harcourt, Brace, 1923.

Bibel und Kirche, III.3 (1983)—issue devoted to depth psychology and biblical expression.

Bishop, J. G. "Psychological Insights in St. Paul's Mysticism." *Theology* 78 (1975): 318–24.

Bolin, Edward P. and Goldberg, Glenn M. "Behavioral Psychology and the Bible: General and Specific Considerations." *Journal of Psychology and Theology* 7 (1979):167–75.

Boyarin, Daniel. *Intertextuality and the Reading of Midrash.* Bloomington/Indianapolis: Indiana University Press, 1990.

Brenner, Athalya. "Female Social Behavior: Two Descriptive Patterns Within the 'Birth of the Hero' Paradigm." *Vetus testamentus* 36 (1986): 257–73.

Brome, Vincent. *Jung.* New York: Atheneum, 1981.

Brown, Peter. *The Body and Society: Men, Women and Sexual Renunciation in Early Christianity.* New York: Columbia University Press, 1988.

Brown, Raymond E. *The Community of the Beloved Disciple.* New York: Paulist, 1979.

————. *The Epistles of John.* AB 30. Garden City: Doubleday, 1981.

Brown, Schuyler. "Universalism and Particularism in Matthew's Gospel." In *SBL Seminar Papers*, ed. D. J. Lull, 388–99. Atlanta: Scholars Press, 1989.

————. "The Beloved Disciple: A Jungian View." In *The Conversation Continues: Studies in Paul and John in Honor of J. Louis Martyn*, ed. R. T. Fortna and B. R. Gaventa, 366–77. Nashville: Abingdon, 1990.

Buber, Martin. "Dark shel miqra." In *The Hebrew Bible in Literary Criticism*, ed. Alex Preminger and Edward Greenstein. New York: Ungar, 1986.

Bufford, R. K. *The Human Reflex: Behavioral Psychology in Biblical Perspective.* San Francisco: Harper and Row, 1981.

Bultmann, Rudolf. *The Gospel of John: A Commentary.* Trans. G. R. Beasley-Murray, et. al. Philadelphia: Westminster, 1971.

Campbell, Joseph. *The Hero with a Thousand Faces.* Princeton: Princeton University, 1973.

Capps, Donald E. *Biblical Approaches to Pastoral Counseling.* Philadelphia: Westminster, 1981.

————. "The Beatitudes and Erikson's Life Cycle Theory." *Pastoral Psychology* 33 (1985): 226–44.

Chavel, Charles B. *Ramban (Nachmanides) Commentary on the Torah: Genesis.* New York: Shilo, 1971.

Clift, Wallace B. *Jung and Christianity: The Challenge of Reconciliation.* New York: Crossroad, 1982.

Clines, David J. A. *The Theme of the Pentateuch.* Journal for the Study of the Old Testament Supplement Series 10. Sheffield: University of Sheffield, 1982.

Corbin, Henry. *Creative Imagination in the Sufism of Ibn 'Arabī.* Trans. R. Manheim. London: Routledge and Kegan Paul, 1970.

————. "*Mundus Imaginalis*, or The Imaginary and the Imaginal." *Spring* 1972: 1–19.

————. "Pour une charte de l'Imaginal." In *Corps spirituel et Terre céleste.* Paris: Editions Buchet/Chastel, 1979.

Cox, David. *Jung and St. Paul: A Study of the Doctrine of Justification by Faith and Its Relation to the Conception of Individuation.* New York: Association Press, 1959.

Crossan, John D. "Perspectives and Methods in Contemporary Biblical Criticism." *Biblical Research* 22 (1977): 39–49.

Culpepper, R. Alan. *Anatomy of the Fourth Gospel: A Study in Literary Design.* Philadelphia: Fortress Press, 1983.

Dallett, Janet. "Active Imagination in Practice." In *Jungian Analysis*, ed. Murray Stein, 173–91. Boston: New Science Library, 1982.

Davidson, Robert. *Genesis 12–50.* Cambridge: University Press, 1979.

Delitzsch, Franz. *A System of Biblical Psychology.* Trans. A. E. Wallis. Grand Rapids: Baker Book House, 1966.

Delormé, J. "Qu'est-ce qui fait courir les éxégetes?" *Lumiére et Vie* 29: 77–89.

Diel, Paul. *The God-Symbol*. San Francisco: Harper and Row, 1986.

———. *Symbolism in the Bible: Its Psychological Significance*. San Francisco: Harper and Row, 1988.

——— and Solotareff, Jeannine. *Symbolism in the Gospel of John*. San Francisco: Harper and Row, 1988.

Dittes, James E. "Analytic (Jungian) Psychology and Religion." In *Dictionary of Pastoral Care and Counseling*, ed. Rodney J. Hunter. Nashville: Abingdon, 1990.

Dolto, Francoise and Sévérin, Gerard. *The Jesus of Psychoanalysis: A Freudian Interpretation of the Gospel*. Garden City: Doubleday, 1978.

———. *The Psyche as a Sacrament: A Comparative Study of C. G. Jung and Paul Tillich*. Toronto: Inner City, 1981.

———. *The Illness That We Are: A Jungian Critique of Christianity*. Toronto: Inner City Books, 1984.

Dourley, John. "The Jung, Buber, White Exchanges: Exercises in Futility." *Studies in Religion* 20 (1991): 299–309.

Drewermann, Eugen. *Strukturen des Bösen*. Paderborner Theologische Studien 4–6. 3 vols. München/Paderborn/Wien: Schöningh, 1981–1982.

———. *Tiefenpsychologie und Exegese*. Vol. 1: *Die Wahrheit der Formen*. Vol. 2: *Der Wahrheit der Werke und Worte. Wunder, Vision, Weissagung, Apokalypse, Geschichte, Gleichnis*. Olten/ Freiburg: Walter, 1984–1985.

Edinger, Edward. *Ego and Archetype: Individuation and the Religious Function of the Psyche*. C. G. Jung Foundation for Analytical Psychology. New York: Putnam, 1972.

———. *The Bible and the Psyche: Individuation Symbolism in the Old Testament*. Toronto: Inner City Books, 1986.

———. *The Christian Archetype: A Jungian Commentary on the Life of Christ*. Toronto: Inner City Books, 1987.

Eilberg-Schwartz, Howard. *Patterns in Comparative Religion*. Trans. Rosemary Sheed. New York: Sheed and Ward, 1958.

———. *Yoga*. Trans. W. Trask. New York: Pantheon, 1958.

———. *Cosmos and History*. Torchbook Edition; New York: Harper and Row, 1959.

———. *Shamanism: Archaic Techniques of Ecstasy*. Trans. Willard Trask. London: Routledge, 1964.

———. *The Savage in Judaism*. Bloomington: Indiana University Press, 1990.

Engelsman, Joan Chamberlain. *The Feminine Dimension of the Divine*. Philadelphia: Westminster, 1978.

Falconer, M. D., W. Clark, and Colin A. Ross, M.D. "The Tilted Family." *Canadian Journal of Psychiatry* 31/7 (1986): 649–52.

Fishbane, Michael. *Text and Texture*. New York: Schocken, 1979.

Fletcher, M. Scott. *The Psychology of the New Testament*. New York: Hodder and Stoughton, 1912.

Fodor, A. "The Fall of Man in the Book of Genesis." *American Imago* 11 (1954): 201–31. Fokkelman, J. P. "Genesis." In *The Literary Guide to the Bible*, ed. Robert Alter and Frank Kermode, 36–55. Cambridge: Belknap Press, 1987.

Freud, Sigmund. *Standard Edition of the Complete Psychological Works*. Trans. J. Strachey London: Hogarth, 1953–1974.

Gaster, Theodor and Patai, Raphael. *Hebrew Myths: The Book of Genesis*. Garden City: Doubleday, 1964.

Goldenberg, Naomi. "Jung after Feminism." In *Beyond Androcentrism: New Essays on Women and Religion*, ed. Rita M. Gross, 53–66. American Academy of Religion Aids for the Study of Religion 6. Missoula: Scholars Press, 1977.

Goodenough, Erwin R. *The Psychology of Religious Experiences*. New York: Basic Books, 1965.

Grant, F. C. "Psychological Study of the Bible." In *Religions in Antiquity (Numen, XIV)*, ed. J. Neusner. Leiden: Brill, 1989.

Greeley, Andrew. "Pop Psychology and the Gospel." *Theology Today* 33 (1976): 224–31.

Gregory, Sadie. *A New Dimension in Old Testament Study: A Course Guide to the Study of Selections from the Old Testament for Individuals and Groups*. San Francisco: Guild for Psychological Studies, 1980.

Guillaumont, A. *The Gospel According to Thomas: Coptic Text Established and Translated*. New York: Harper and Row, 1959.

Halperin, David. *Seeking Ezekiel: Text and Psychology*. State College: Penn State Press, 1991.

Hartman, L. and von Imschoot, P. *Encyclopedic Dictionary of the Bible*. New York: McGraw Hill, 1963.

Healer, C. T. *Freud and St. Paul*. Philadelphia: Dorrance, 1972.

Hedrick, C. W. and Hodgson Jr., R., eds. *Nag Hammadi, Gnosticism, and Early Christianity* Peabody, Mass: Hendrickson Publishers, 1986.

Hendel, Ronald S. *The Epic of the Patriarch: The Jacob Cycle and the Narrative Traditions of Caanan and Israel*. Harvard Semitic Monographs 42. Atlanta: Scholars Press, 1987.

Hillman, James. *Archetypal Psychology*. Dallas: Spring Publications, 1983.

Holmberg, Bengt. *Sociology and the New Testament: An Appraisal*. Minneapolis: Fortress, 1990.

Homans, Peter. "Psychology and Hermeneutics: Jung's Contribution." *Zygon* 4 (1969): 333–55.

Hora, Thomas. *Existential Metapsychiatry*. New York: Seabury Press, 1977.

Howes, Elizabeth B. and Moon, Sheila. *The Choicemaker*. Wheaton, Ill: Theosophical Publishing House, 1977.

Jacobi, Jolande. *The Way of Individuation.* Trans. R. F. C. Hull. New York: Harcourt, Brace, 1967.

———. *The Psychology of C. G. Jung.* New Haven: Yale University Press, 1971.

Jaffé, Aniela, ed. *C. G. Jung: Word and Image.* Princeton: Princeton University Press, 1979.

Jone, Ernest. "Eine Psychoanalytische Studie über den Heiligen Geist." *Imago* 9 (1928): 58–72.

Jung, C. G. *The Collected Works of C. G. Jung.* Ed. G. Adler, M. Fordham, Sir H. Read, and W. McGuire. Trans. by R. F. C. Hull. Vols. I–XX. Princeton: Princeton University Press, 1953–79. These works are cited in the footnotes by volume number and paragraph (rather than page) number.

———. *Memories, Dreams, Reflections.* Ed. Aniela Jaffé. Trans. R. and C. Winston. New York: Pantheon, 1963.

———. *Man and His Symbols.* Garden City: Doubleday, 1964.

———. *Psychological Reflections.* Ed. J. Jacobi. Trans. R. F. C. Hull. Princeton: Princeton University Press, 1970.

———. *Letters.* 2 vols. Ed. G. Adler, A. Jaffé. Trans. R. F. C. Hull. Princeton: Princeton University Press, 1973, 1975.

———. *The Visions Seminars.* 2 vols. Zürich: Spring Publications, 1976.

———. *The Zofingia Lectures.* Ed. William McGuire. Princeton: Princeton University Press, 1983.

———. *Analytical Psychology: Notes of the Seminar Given in 1925 by C. G. Jung.* Ed. William McGuire. Princeton: Princeton University Press, 1989.

Kassel, Maria. *Biblische Urbilder: Tiefenpsychologische Auslegung nach C. G. Jung.* Pfeiffer Werbücher 147. München: Pfeiffer, 1982.

Kelsey, Morton. *Christo-psychology.* New York: Crossroad, 1982.

———. *Dreams: The Dark Speech of the Spirit.* Garden City: Doubleday, 1988.

Kerr, Hugh T. "The Christ-Life as Mythic and Psychic Symbol." *The Princeton Seminary Bulletin* 55: 25–34.

Kingsland, W. *The Gnosis or Ancient Wisdom in the Christian Scriptures.* London: Allen and Unwin, 1954.

Kluger, H. Yechezel. "Ruth: A Contribution to the Feminine Principle in the Old Testament." *Spring* (1957): 52–88.

Kluger, Rivkah Scharf. *Satan in the Old Testament.* Evanston: Northwestern University Press, 1967.

———. *Psyche and Bible: Three Old Testament Themes.* Zürich: Spring, 1974.

Koehler-Baumgartner. *Lexicon in Veteris Testamenti Libros.* Leiden: Brill, 1953.

Krieger, Murray. *A Window to Criticism: Shakespeare's Sonnets and Modern Poetics.* Princeton: Princeton University Press, 1964.

Kristeva, Julia. *Powers of Horror.* New York: Columbia University Press, 1982.

Kühlwein, J. "Gotteserfahrung und Reifungsgeschicte in der Jakob-Esau- Erzählung." *Werden und Wirken des Alten Testaments: Festschrift fur Claus Westermann Zum 70. Geburtstag.* Ed. Rainer Albertz; Hans-Peter Mueller; Hans Walter Wolff; and Walther Zimmerli. Göttingen: Vandenhoeck and Ruprecht, 1980.

Kühlewind, Georg. *Becoming Aware of the Logos: The Way of St. John the Evangelist.* Trans. F. and J. Schwarzkopf. Great Barrington: Lindisfarne Press, 1985.

Kümmel, Werner George. *The New Testament: The History of the Investigation of Its Problems.* Trans. S. MacLean Gilmour and Howard Clark Kee. Nashville: Abingdon, 1972.

Kysar, Robert. "Johannine Metaphor—Meaning and Function: A Literary Case Study of John 10:1–8." *Semeia* 53 (1991): 81–111.

L'Heureux, Conrad E. *Life Journey and the Old Testament: An Experiential Approach to the Bible and Personal Transformation.* New York: Paulist Press, 1986.

Lang, Bernard. *Drewermann, Interprète de la Bible.* Paris: Les Éditions du Cerf, 1994.

Leon-Dufour, Xavier. "Towards a Symbolic Reading of the Fourth Gospel." *NTS* 27 (1980–81): 439–56.

Lévy, Ludwig. "Sexualsymbolik in der Simonsage." *Zeitschrift für Sexualwissenschaft* 2 (1916): 256–71.

———. "Sexualsymbolik in der biblischen Paradiesgeschichte." *Imago* 5 (1917–18): 16–30.

Lowe, James H., ed. *"Rashi" on the Pentateuch: Genesis.* London: Hebrew Compendium Publishing, 1928.

Lüdemann, G. *Untersuchungen zur simonianischen Gnosis.* Göttingen: Vandenhoeck and Ruprecht, 1975.

McGann, Diarmund. *The Journeying Self: The Gospel of Mark Through a Jungian Perspective.* New York: The Paulist Press, 1985.

MacRae, George. "The Fourth Gospel and Religionsgeschichte." *CBQ* 32 (1970): 13–24.

Malina, Bruce. *The New Testament World: A Cultural Anthropological Approach.* Atlanta: John Knox, 1981.

Martyn, J. Louis. *History and Theology in the Fourth Gospel.* Nashville: Abingdon, 1979.

Meeks, Wayne. "The Man from Heaven in Johannine Sectarianism." *JBL* 91 (1972): 44–72.

Merkur, Daniel, "The Visionary Practice of Jewish Apocalyptists." In *The Psychoanalytical Study of Society*, vol. 14, ed. L. B. Boyer and S. A. Grognick, 119–48. Hillsdale: The Analytic Press, 1989.

Meves, Christa. *The Bible Answers Us with Pictures.* Trans. Hal Taussig. Philadelphia: Westminster, 1977.

Miller, David L. "Theology's Ego/Religion's Soul." *Spring* (1980): 78–88.

———. *Christs: Meditations on Archetypal Images in Christian Theology.* New York: Seabury, 1981.

———. *Three Faces of God: Traces of the Trinity in Literature and Life.* Philadelphia: Fortress Press, 1987.

———. *Hells and Holy Ghosts: A Theopoetics of Christian Belief.* Nashville: Abingdon, 1989.

Miller, Donald and Snyder, Gradon and Neff, Robert. *Using Biblical Simulations.* Valley Forge: Judson Press, 1973.

Miller, John W. "Psychoanalytic Approaches to Biblical Religion." *Journal of Religion and Health* 22 (1983): 19–29.

Miller, William T. *Mysterious Encounters at Mamre and Jabbok.* Brown Judaic Studies 50. Ed. Jacob Neusner. Chico: Scholars Press, 1984.

Miller, Patricia Cox. *Dreams in Late Antiquity: Studies in the Imagination of a Culture.* Princeton: Princeton University Press, 1994.

Moore, Robert L. "Pauline Theology and the Return of the Repressed: Depth Psychology and Early Christian Thought." *Zygon* 13 (1978): 158–68.

Moore, Stephen D. *Literary Criticism and the Gospels: The Theoretical Challenge.* New Haven: Yale University Press, 1989.

Morgan, R. and Barton, J. *Biblical Interpretation.* London: Oxford University Press, 1988.

Neill, Stephen. *The Interpretation of the New Testament 1861–1961.* London: Oxford University Press, 1964.

Neumann, Erich. *The Origins and History of Consciousness.* Princeton: Princeton University Press, 1971.

———. *Depth Psychology and a New Ethic.* New York: Harper and Row, 1973.

Neyrey, Jerome R. *An Ideology of Revolt: Johannine Christology in Social-Science Perspective.* Philadelphia: Fortress, 1988.

Niederwimmer, Kurt. "Tiefenpsychologie und Exegese." In *Perspektiven der Pastoralpsychologie,* ed. Richard Riesse, 63–78. Göttingen: Vandenhoeck and Ruprecht, 1974.

Oates, Wayne E. *The Bible in Pastoral Care.* Philadelphia: Westminster, Philipson, Morris, 1953.

Origen. *On First Principles.* New York: Harper and Row, 1966.

Painter, John. "Johannine Symbols: A Case Study in Epistemology." *Journal of Theology for Southern Africa* 27 (1979): 26–41.

Pfister, Oskar, "Die Entwicklung des Apostels Paulus: Eine religions-geshichtliche und psychologische Skizze." *Imago* 6 (1920): 243–80.

Philip, H. L. *Freud and Religious Belief.* New York: Pitman Publishing Corporation, 1956.

Philipson, Morris. *Outline of a Jungian Aesthetics.* Evanston: Northwestern University Press, 1963.

Plaut, W. Gunther. *The Torah: A Modern Commentary.* Vol. I, *Genesis.* New York: Union of American Hebrew Congregations, 1974.

Pruyser, Paul. "Nathan and David: A Psychological Footnote." *Pastoral Psychology* 13 (1962): 14–18.

———. "Life and Death of a Symbol: A History of the Holy Ghost Concept and its Symbols." *McCormick Quarterly* 18 Special Supplement (1985): 5–22.

Reik, Theodor. "Psychoanalytic Studies of Bible Exegesis, I: The Wrestling of Jacob." In *Dogma and Compulsion.* New York: International Universities Press, 1951.

———. "The Face of God." *Psychoanalysis* 3 (1955): 3–28.

———. *Mystery on the Mountain: The Drama of the Sinai Revelation.* New York: Harper and Row, 1958.

———. *The Creation of Woman: A Psychoanalytic Inquiry into the Myth of Eve.* New York, Braziller, 1960.

———. *The Temptation.* New York: Braziller, 1961.

Rensberger, David. *Johannine Faith and Liberating Community.* Philadelphia: Westminster, 1987.

Robinson, H. Wheeler. "The Psychology of Inspiration." In *Inspiration and Revelation in the Old Testament.* Oxford: Clarendon, 1946.

Robinson, J. M., ed. *The Nag Hammadi Library.* San Francisco: Harper and Row, 1988.

Róheim, Géza. "The Garden of Eden." *Psychoanalytic Review* 27 (1940): 1–26, 177–99.

Rollins, W. G. *Jung and the Bible.* Atlanta: John Knox Press, 1983.

———. "Jung on Scripture and Hermeneutics: Retrospect and Project." In *Essays on Jung and the Study of Religion,* ed. L. H. Martin and J. Goss. New York: University Press of America, 1985.

———. "Jung's Challenge to Biblical Hermeneutics." In *Jung's Challenge to Contemporary Religion,* ed. M. Stein and R. Moore. Wilmette: Chiron Publications, 1986.

Rubenstein, Richard. *My Brother Paul.* New York: Harper and Row, 1972.

Rudolph, K. *Gnosis: The Nature and History of Gnosticism.* Trans. R. M. Wilson. New York: Harper and Row, 1987.

Sales, M. (S.J.). "Possibilités et limites d'une lecture psychoanalytique de la Bible." *Nouvelle Revue Théologique* (Tournai) 101 (1979): 699–723.

Sanday, William. *Personality in Christ and in Ourselves.* Oxford: Clarendon, 1911.

Sanford, John. *Dreams: God's Forgotten Language.* Philadelphia: Lippincott, 1968.

———. *The Man who Wrestled with God.* King of Prussia: Religious Publishing Co., 1974.

———. *Evil: The Shadow Side of Reality*. New York: Crossroad, 1982.

———. *King Saul, The Tragic Hero*. New York: Paulist Press, 1985.

———. *The Kingdom Within: The Inner Meaning of Jesus' Sayings*. San Francisco: Harper and Row, 1986.

———. "Jesus, Paul and Depth Psychology." *Religious Education* 68: 673–89.

Sarna, Nahum M. *Understanding Genesis*. New York: Schocken Books, 1966.

Schüssler Fiorenza, Elisabeth. *In Memory of Her: A Feminist Theological Reconstruction*. New York: Crossroad, 1984.

Schwartz-Salant, Nathan. "Patriarchy in Transformation: Judaic, Christian, and Clinical Perspectives." In *Jung's Challenge to Contemporary Religion*, ed. Murray Stein and Robert L. Moore. Wilmette: Chiron Publications, 1987.

Schweitzer, Albert. *The Psychiatric Study of Jesus: Exposition and Criticism*. Trans. Charles R. Joy Boston: Beacon Press, 1948.

Scroggs, Robin. "The Heuristic Value of a Psychoanalytic Model in the Interpretation of Pauline Theology." *Zygon* 13 (1978): 136–57.

———. *Paul for a New Day*. Philadelphia: Fortress, 1977.

———. "The Sociological Interpretation of the New Testament: The Present State of Research." *NTS* 26 (1980): 166.

———. "Psychology as a Tool to Interpret the Text." *Christian Century* (March 24, 1982): 335–38.

Segal, Robert A. "Jung and Gnosticism." *Religion* 17 (1987): 301–36.

Segovia, Fernando F. "Towards a New Direction in Johannine Scholarship: The Fourth Gospel from a Literary Perspective," and "The Final Farewell of Jesus: A Reading of John 20:30–21:25." *Semeia* 53 (1991): 1–112, 167–90.

Singer, June. *Boundaries of the Soul: The Practice of Jung's Psychology*. Garden City: Doubleday, 1972.

———. *Androgyny: Towards a New Theory of Sexuality*. Garden City, N.Y.: Anchor Press/Doubleday, 1977.

Slochower, Harry. "The Book of Job: The Hebrew Myth of the Chosen God, its Symbolism and Psychoanalytic Process." *The International Record of Medicine* 171/12 (1958): 761–70.

Smith, J. Z. "Adde parvum parvo magnus acervus erit." In *Map Is Not the Territory*, 240–64. Leiden: Brill, 1978.

———. "In Comparison a Magic Dwells." In *Imagining Religion*, 19–35. Chicago: University of Chicago Press, 1982.

———. *Drudgery Divine*. Chicago: University of Chicago Press, 1990.

———. *Differential Equations*. Tempe: Arizona State University Department of Religion, 1992.

Smith, Richard. "Afterword: The Modern Relevance of Gnosticism." In *The Nag Hammadi Library*, ed. J. M. Robinson. San Francisco: Harper and Row, 1988.

Speiser, E. *Genesis.* AB 1. Garden City: Doubleday, 1964.

Spiegel, Yorick, ed. *Psychoanalytische Interpretationen Biblischer Texte.* München: Kaiser, 1972.

Stein, Dominique. "Une lecture psychoanalytique de la Bible." *Revue des Sciences Philosophiques et Théologiques* 72 (1988): 95–108.

Stein, Murray. *Jung's Treatment of Christianity: The Psychotherapy of a Religious Tradition.* Wilmette: Chiron Publications, 1985.

Strickman, H. N. and Silver, Arthur M., eds. *Ibn Ezra's Commentary on the Pentateuch: Genesis (Bereshit).* New York: Menorah, 1988.

Taylor, Vincent. *The Person of Christ in New Testament Teaching.* London: Macmillan, 1959.

Tenzler, J. "Tiefenpsychologie und Wunderfrage." *Münchener Theologische Zeitschrift* 25 (1974): 118–37.

Theissen, Gerd. *Psychologische Aspekte Paulinischer Theologie.* Göttingen: Vandenhoeck und Ruprecht, 1983.

——. *Psychological Aspects of Pauline Theology.* Trans. John P. Galvin. Minneapolis: Fortress, 1987.

Tolbert, Mary Ann. "The Prodigal Son: A Reading from a Psychoanalytic Perspective." *Semeia* 9 (1977):1–20.

——. *Perspectives on the Parables: An Approach to Multiple Interpretations.* Phildelphia: Fortress, 1978.

——. "A Response from a Literary Perspective." *Semeia* 53 (1991): 203–12.

Trible, Phyllis. *God and the Rhetoric of Sexuality.* Philadelphia: Fortress Press, 1978.

Uleyn, A. J. R. "The Possessed Man of Gerasa: A Psychoanalytic Interpretation of Reader Reactions." In *Current Issues in Psychology of Religion,* ed. J. Belzen and J. Lans, 90–96. Amsterdam: Rodopi, 1986.

Vawter, Bruce. *A Path Through Genesis.* New York: Sheed and Ward, 1956.

——. *On Genesis: A New Reading.* Garden City: Doubleday, 1977.

Vergote, Antoine, "Apports des données psychanalytiques a l'exégése." In *Exégése et herméneutique.* Paris: Éditions du Seuil, 1971.

——. "Psychanalyse et interprétation biblique." In *Supplément au dictionnaire de la Bible,* 9: 252–60. Paris, 1979.

Via, Dan. "The Prodigal Son: A Jungian Reading," *Semeia* 9 (1977): 21–43.

Von Franz, M.-L. *Alchemy: An Introduction to the Symbolism and the Psychology.* Toronto: Inner City Books, 1980.

Von Rad, Gerhard. "The Joseph Narrative and Ancient Wisdom." In *The Problem of the Hexateuch.* New York: McGraw Hill, 1966.

Wehr, Gerhard. *Jung: A Biography.* Trans. David M. Weeks. Boston: Shambhala Publications, 1988.

Wellisch, E. *Isaac and Oedipus: A Study in Biblical Psychology of the Sacrifice of Isaac.* London, 1954.

Werblowsky, R. J. Z. "Structure and Archetypes." *Journal of the Ancient Near Eastern Society of Columbia University* 5 (1973): 435–42.

Wernik, Uri. "Frustrated Beliefs and Early Christianity: A Psychological Inquiry into the Gospels of the New Testament." *Numen* 22 (1975): 96–130.

Westman, Heinz. *The Structure of Biblical Myths: The Ontogensis of the Psyche.* Dallas: Spring Publications, 1983.

———. *The Springs of Creativity: The Bible and the Creative Process of the Psyche.* Wilmette: Chiron Publications, 1988.

Wiesel, Elie. *Messengers of God.* New York: Random House, 1976.

Willett, Michael E. "Jung and John." *Explorations* 77 (Fall 1988): 77–92.

———. *Wisdom Christology in the Fourth Gospel.* San Francisco: Mellen Research University Press, 1992.

Wink, Walter. *The Bible in Human Transformation: Toward a New Paradigm for Biblical Study.* Philadelphia: Fortress Press, 1973.

———. "On Wrestling with God: Using Psychological Insights in Biblical Study." *Religion in Life* 47 (1978): 136–47.

———. *Transforming Bible Study: A Leader's Guide.* Nashville: Abingdon, 1980.

———. *Naming the Powers: The Language of Power in the New Testament.* Philadelphia: Fortress Press, 1984.

———. *Unmasking the Powers: The Invisible Forces that Determine Human Existence.* Philadelphia: Fortress Press, 1986.

———. *Engaging the Powers: Discernement and Resistance in a World of Domination.* Minneapolis: Fortress Press, 1992.

Wise, Carroll A. *Psychiatry and the Bible.* New York: Harper and Row, 1956.

Wolff, Werner. *Changing Concepts of the Bible: A Psychological Analysis of Its Words, Symbols, and Beliefs.* New York: Hermitage, 1951.

Wuellner, Wilhelm. "Where is Rhetorical Criticism Taking Us?" *The Catholic Biblical Quarterly* 49 (1987): 448–63.

———. "Putting Life back into the Lazarus Story." *Semeia* 53 (1991): 113–32.

——— and Leslie, Robert C. *The Surprising Gospel: Intriguing Psychological Insights from the New Testament.* Nashville: Abingdon Press, 1984.

Zeligs, Dorothy F. "Two Episodes in the Life of Jacob." *American Imago* 10 (1953): 181–203.

———. "A Character Study of Samuel." *American Imago* 12 (1955): 355–88.

———. "The Personality of Joseph." *American Imago* 12 (1955): 47–69.

———. "Saul, The Tragic King." *American Imago* 14 (1957): 81–85, 164–89.

———. *Moses: A Psychodynamic Study.* New York: Human Sciences Press, 1986.

———. *Psychoanalysis and the Bible: A Study in Depth of Seven Leaders.* New York: Human Sciences Press, 1988.